Where Did
Shakespeare
Get His Ideas?

© 2017 Simon Webb

The right of Simon Webb to be identified as the Author of the Work has been asserted by him in accordance with the Copyright, Designs and Patents Act 1988.

All rights reserved.

First published by The Langley Press, 2017

This book is an abridged version, without parallel passages, of the 2015 Langley Press book *The Sources of Shakespeare's Plays: An Introduction*

The cover shows *Apollo and the Muses* by Claude Lorrain (Getty Museum)

Also from The Langley Press:

Aubrey's *Brief Lives*: Omibus Edition

The History of King Richard III by Thomas More

Love Sonnets of Dante and His Circle Translated by Dante Gabriel Rossetti

Chaucer' *Parliament of Fowls* in a Modern English Verse Translation

The Voyage of Saint Brendan

Bede's *Life of St Cuthbert*

A Book for Valentine's Day

Nicholas Breakspear: The Pope from England

Aaron of Lincoln

For free downloads and more from the Langley Press, visit our website at: http://tinyurl.com/lpdirect

Where Did
Shakespeare
Get His Ideas?

by

Simon Webb

Contents

I. Shakespeare's Alchemy	9
II. Richard III	48
III. The Tempest	68
IV. Antony and Cleopatra	104
Afterword: Sources for the Sources	124
Bibliography	126

*For my friend and fellow
Shakespeare enthusiast,
Theo Harman*

I. Shakespeare's Alchemy

In March 2012 a team of very well-equipped experts descended on the Folger Shakespeare Library at 201 East Capitol Street, Washington DC. Among other equipment, they brought a digital camera fitted with a '39-megapixel monochrome digital sensor', and some devices called 'spectral illumination panels'.

Despite the appearance of the phrase 'spectral illumination' in the last paragraph, readers should not suppose that the visitors were trying to illuminate any ghosts, such as the spirits of the library's founders, Henry and Emily Folger. The purpose of the two-day visit was to take high-tech pictures of a small corner of one page of a dilapidated sixteenth-century volume, that has been in the library since 1938.

The book is one of the library's copies of

Archaionomia by William Lambarde, published in 1568. It has sections in Latin, and in Old English, a language otherwise known as Anglo-Saxon, which was spoken in England before the Norman Conquest. The book is interesting as it is only the second book printed in England to use the Old English alphabet, which differs from the modern English alphabet. *Archaionomia* has pages of Old English with Latin translations on facing pages, and it also has some historical material relating to Anglo-Saxon times, together with a map of the seven kingdoms of Anglo-Saxon England. This map may be the first ever to be designed, engraved, printed and published in England.

Lambarde's *Archaionomia* is primarily about the ancient laws of Anglo-Saxon England, and much of its text is derived from a transcript of a manuscript, held in the British Library in London, which is now over a thousand years old. Although the subject-matter of *Archaionomia* may sound a little dry to readers with no interest in, for instance, the laws passed under King Canute, it was a popular book in the sixteenth century, and was even used by lawyers to bolster their arguments in court-cases.

It was not really the intrinsic appeal of

Archaionomia that brought the experts with their cunning devices to the Folger in 2012, however. What they were interested in was a signature just visible in the top-right-hand corner of the title page. This signature is thought to be that of the playwright William Shakespeare, and the Folger's copy number seven of *Archaionomia* may be the only surviving copy of a book for which we have evidence of Shakespeare's personal ownership.

In a 1992 article in the journal *Shakespeare Quarterly*, Giles Dawson recounts how this potentially very interesting volume was bought from Sotheby's auction house by the Folger, together with three other books, in a single auction lot in 1938, for just £2. In today's money, that would be the equivalent of around £74, or 110 US dollars. A remarkable feature of the sale was that two of the books in the lot, including *Archaionomia,* were not even named in the catalogue.

What may be Shakespeare's signature was not even spotted by the people at the Folger until the book was sent to be re-bound. It was the bookbinder who found the signature, which is hard to spot because the ink has faded, and in any case the signature was written over the decorative border of the title-page. The signature is only really visible on the *back* of the title-page, where the ink has soaked through. Here, of course, the signature is reversed, and can only be appreciated properly if a mirror is held up to it.

In his 1992 article, Dawson shows how, having compared this signature to others thought to be Shakespeare's, he determined that the signature on *Archaionomia* appears to be genuine. He also makes the point that if a forger had applied the signature, he would surely not have put it on a decorative border, where it would have been hard to discern even when the ink wasn't yet dry.

The present author would add that if a forger had wanted to pass off an old book as one that had been owned by Shakespeare, he would surely have picked a book that the playwright is known to have used. Obvious candidates would include the *Metamorphoses* of Ovid, and Holinshed's Chronicle.

Even if Shakespeare's signature on this copy of *Archaionomia* is genuine, there is no guarantee that the playwright ever read the book; although it is possible that he did read it, and that it had an influence on his writing. In his Latin dedication, Lambarde remarks that 'no nation was ever conquered that had not first suffered disorder from its enemies within'. He later says that the laws of England are 'like a wall built of stone and oak to defend a city'.

Neither of these are very original observations, but both are lessons that might be learned by a reader of Shakespeare's plays. In *Hamlet*, Denmark is under threat from Norway because the Norwegian prince Fortinbras thinks that the Danish state might have been weakened by the death of Old Hamlet. Likewise, in Act I scene 3 of *Antony and Cleopatra*, Antony, who is beginning to see himself as a weak element in the Roman power structure, tells us that 'Our Italy| Shines o'er with civil swords,' one consequence of which is that Sextus Pompeius dares to make 'his approaches to the port of Rome', in a bid to take over from the trio of men who then ruled the Roman empire.

But the closest Shakespeare gets to Lambarde's idea of the law acting as a wall is in Act III, scene 4 of *Richard II*, where one of the gardener's servants asks:

> Why should we in the compass of a pale
> Keep law and form and due proportion,
> Showing, as in a model, our firm estate,
> When our sea-walled garden, the whole land, Is full of weeds

This does not, however, liken the law itself to a defensive wall.

Although some unoriginal thoughts might be echoed, there is very little else to connect Lambarde's *Archaionomia* to Shakespeare's plays. Shakespeare never wrote a play set in Anglo-Saxon England: his legendary British kings, Lear and Cymbeline, date from pre-Roman and Roman times respectively; and after Cymbeline, who is supposed to have lived at the time of Jesus, the playwright jumps twelve centuries and lands on King John.

The one reference to William Lambarde in Kenneth Muir's book *The Sources of Shakespeare's Plays* connects him with the chronicler Raphael Holinshed, the antiquaries William Camden and John Stow, and the magician John Dee. Muir suggests that Shakespeare may have been acquainted with all of these men, and could have followed up references in their works by asking them questions; and also gained access to obscure manuscript sources by borrowing from their libraries. If it is true that Shakespeare knew Lambarde, then his copy of *Archaionomia* may have been a gift from the author.

Another link between Lambarde and Shakespeare is implied in a strange little story about an encounter between Lambarde and Queen Elizabeth I at Greenwich in August 1601. The story was printed by John Nicol in his book *Bibliotheca Topographica Britannica* (1780).

On this occasion, Lambarde presented the queen with his *Pandecta Ratulorum*, a historical survey of the royal archives then kept at the Tower of London (Lambarde had been appointed Keeper of these records earlier that year).

It seems that Elizabeth did not regard this presentation as a mere formal ceremony: she flicked through the *Pandecta* and asked questions about it. Soon she 'fell upon the reign of King Richard II' and stated 'I am Richard II: know ye not that?'

Lambarde immediately understood why the queen said this: she was referring to the failed rebellion led by Robert Devereaux, the earl of Essex, that had taken place a few months earlier. A feature of this rebellion had been a special performance of Shakespeare's *Richard II* at the Globe Theatre, that had been arranged by Essex's followers. The performance had included the scene (Act IV, scene 1) where Richard hands over his crown to the usurper Henry Bolingbroke: a politically sensitive scene that had almost certainly not been performed in public before, and which had been excluded from the 1597 printed edition of the play. Months later at Greenwich, Elizabeth was remembering how the rebels had tried to use the deposition of Richard II to persuade the people that it was possible for Elizabeth herself to be deposed.

In her conversation with Lambarde, Elizabeth went on to state that 'this tragedy was played forty times in open streets and houses'. It is possible that the queen, who was then approaching seventy, had become a little confused about this: the rebels had paid *forty shillings* for their special performance of *Richard II*: equivalent to over £200 today. It seems unlikely that anything like forty performances of *Richard II* could have been staged at the time of the rebellion.

We do not have an inventory of Shakespeare's personal library, and no books were mentioned in the will he had drawn up in 1616, the year of his death. Except in the case of *Archaionomia* (and the authenticity of that signature has been disputed) we can only find out what Shakespeare read by considering certain known aspects of his life, and by studying his plays and poems for clues to their sources. Scholars have been fishing for Shakespeare's sources in this way for centuries, and they have landed a number of texts that he *must* have read (or at least heard acted or read aloud) and a much larger number of texts which he *probably* knew. There are also texts that he *might* have known.

Speculating on what texts Shakespeare probably knew, or might have read, naturally involves comparing his written works to works that may have been available to him; but there are obvious weaknesses in this procedure. We can get a good idea of what was available to Shakespeare by looking through books that had been printed before certain relevant dates, but we do not have copies of all the books known to have been printed in the fifteenth, sixteenth and seventeenth centuries; and even the records of what was printed (which include many works that are now lost) cannot be complete.

And printed books were by no means all that people read in those days. Many books were circulated in manuscript, and though they were sometimes re-copied by many people for personal use, these are less likely to be extant today. The process of appearing in print has ensured the survival of many texts from Shakespeare's time, simply because the number of copies printed means that, even after hundreds of years, a few still remain. Just one surviving copy of a book from, say, 1600, is enough to allow a modern publisher to produce a new edition, and thus give the old text another helping of immortality.

Shakespeare was aware of the immortality that print could bestow on a writer: this is the opening of his sonnet number fifty-five:

Not marble, nor the gilded monuments
Of princes, shall outlive this powerful rhyme

He was also aware that works neglected by printers and players could fall into obscurity. In Act III scene 2 of *Hamlet* the hero tells us about a play that:

> ... was never acted, or if it was, not above once; for the play, I remember, pleas'd not the million, 'twas caviare to the general. But it was, as I receiv'd it – and others, whose judgements in such matters cried in the top of mine – an excellent play, well digested in the scenes, set down with as much modesty as cunning.

This play, which is mentioned during a conversation about the nature of theatre in general, may be similar to many plays Shakespeare read or watched, which 'pleas'd not the million', were never printed, and are now long-lost.

At least one part of Shakespeare's own output existed for years in manuscript form before it was printed. Although Shakespeare's sonnets are known to have been around much earlier, they were not published until 1609. Long before that, Francis Meres referred to them, in his book *Palladis Tamia* (1598) as 'his [Shakespeare's] sugar'd sonnets among his private friends', suggesting that they were circulating around the members of some kind of Shakespearian coterie for a decade or more before they were ever printed.

Hunting for texts Shakespeare may have known and used, the investigator must, therefore, bear in mind that much of what the playwright may have read is now irretrievably lost; but there is another problem which may be called the opposite of the 'missing source' problem. In some areas, there are *too many* texts from which the playwright might have drawn a particular idea, and it is therefore difficult to pick out a single text which might have acted as a source.

There is a good example of this in one of Shakespeare's history plays. A reference to 'Ephesians' in Act II scene 2 *Henry IV Part II* would seem to suggest that the author was familiar with the Epistle to the Ephesians in the New Testament:

PRINCE HENRY
Well, thus we play the fools with the time, and the spirits of the wise sit in the clouds and mock us. Is your master here in London?

BARDOLPH
Yea, my lord.

PRINCE HENRY
Where sups he? doth the old boar feed in the old frank?

BARDOLPH
At the old place, my lord, in Eastcheap.

PRINCE HENRY
What company?

PAGE
Ephesians, my lord, of the old church.

PRINCE HENRY
Sup any women with him?

PAGE
None, my lord, but old Mistress Quickly and Mistress Doll Tearsheet.

PRINCE HENRY
What pagan may that be?

In this scene, Prince Henry is asking Bardolph (a red-faced thief) and the Page about their master, his old drinking-companion, the adipose-rich knight Sir John Falstaff. The Page tells Henry that Falstaff is supping with 'Ephesians of the old church', which from the context would seem to mean people who are behaving as the Ephesian Christians did before their conversion to Christianity; when they walked:

in vanity of their mind, having their understanding darkened, and being strangers from the life of God through the ignorance that is in them, because of the hardness of their heart: which being past feeling, have given themselves unto wantonness, to work all uncleanness, even with greediness.

(from Ephesians IV, 17-19)

It is clear that Prince Henry understands the Page's reference to the Ephesians, and that he takes 'the old church' to mean paganism, because he asks of Falstaff's new companion Doll Tearsheet, 'What pagan may that be?' ('Pagan' *was* used as a word for a prostitute, but there were plenty of other words that Shakespeare could have chosen.)

Even before the Page's mention of the Ephesians, the author may have been thinking of the New Testament Epistle: Prince Henry says 'the spirits of the wise sit in the clouds and mock us', which recalls Ephesians II, 6: 'And [God] hath raised us up together, and made us sit together in the heavenly places in Christ Jesus'.

It may seem odd that a humble page should make a Biblical reference like this (which must go right over the heads of many modern readers) but Shakespeare may merely have been suggesting an alternative to the once-common practice of calling sinners 'Corinthians'; a reference to another New Testament Epistle. Prince Henry refers to himself as a Corinthian in *Henry IV Part I* (II, 4) and the Oxford English Dictionary records an example of this usage from 1575, over twenty years before Shakespeare wrote his Henry IV plays.

In the Epistle to the Ephesians, which was probably written some time after 62 A.D., Saint Paul (or more likely another author) encourages the Christian community at Ephesus (now a ruined city in modern Turkey) to continue to grow in their faith; and reminds them not to slip back into the wicked paths they followed before they were converted.

As such, the Epistle seems relevant to the action of the Henry IV plays, because in these we see Prince Hal, the son and heir of King Henry IV, learning from his time spent with the sack-drinking, womanising Falstaff, before casting off his lowlife companions and embracing his royal destiny. In the following passage (from Ephesians IV, 22-24) the author instructs his readers in a way that would seem to be particularly relevant to the story of Hal's transformation into Henry V:

. . . cast off, concerning the conversation in time past, that old man, which is corrupt through the deceivable lusts, and be renewed in the spirit of your mind, and put on the new man, which after God is created unto righteousness, and true holiness.

Clearly the Bible translator means by 'that old man' the believer's previous, corrupt self; but Shakespeare, with his poet's eye for double meanings, might have thought of 'that old man' as a specific person, a character he was about to create, to personify wicked worldliness.

That this passage contains an idea that Shakespeare added to the character of Falstaff is possible, even likely. The only other time the word 'Ephesian' is used in Shakespeare to characterise someone who is not actually from the city of Ephesus is in *The Merry Wives of Windsor*, where Falstaff appears again, and where the Host calls to him:

Bully knight! bully Sir John! speak from thy

lungs military: art thou there? it is thine host, thine Ephesian, calls. (IV, 5)

The term 'old man' appears in *Henry IV Part II* in the heart-breaking scene (V, 5) where Henry, now King Henry V, rejects Falstaff:

FALSTAFF
My king! my Jove! I speak to thee, my heart!

HENRY V
I know thee not, old man. Fall to thy prayers.
How ill white hairs become a fool and jester!
I have long dreamt of such a kind of man,
So surfeit-swell'd, so old, and so profane;
But being awak'd, I do despise my dream.
Make less thy body hence, and more thy grace;
Leave gormandizing; know the grave doth gape
For thee thrice wider than for other men—
Reply not to me with a fool-born jest;
Presume not that I am the thing I was,
For God doth know, so shall the world perceive,
That I have turn'd away my former self;
So will I those that kept me company.

It is interesting that Henry's devastating speech to his old friend follows a pagan reference: Falstaff refers to Henry as 'my Jove'. What comes next is deeply Christian, and has much that can be traced to the Epistle to the Ephesians. Henry tells us that his time with Falstaff was like a dream from which he has now awoken: at chapter five verse fourteen, the author of the Epistle tells the Ephesians; 'Awake thou that sleepest, and stand up from the dead'. The new king goes on to warn Falstaff not to reply to him 'with a fool-born jest', recalling the Epistle's command that the faithful should not name 'foolish talking, neither jesting, which are things not comely'.

Some of the specific sins which the author of Ephesians tells the faithful to avoid (or not slip back into) are also reminiscent of Falstaff's way of life; fornication, drunkenness and theft being among them. Indeed the Epistle's idea of the wicked life as a kind of death-like sleep may explain why sleeping at odd hours is one of the first sins we learn that Falstaff commits. In Act I, scene 2 of *Henry IV Part I* Prince Henry tells the knight that he has grown 'fat-witted, with drinking of old sack and unbuttoning thee after supper and sleeping upon benches after noon'. Later in the same play (II, 4) we find Falstaff 'Fast asleep behind the arras, and snorting like a horse'.

Although the Epistle to the Ephesians

may have been Shakespeare's ultimate source for at least one idea from which he constructed the character of Falstaff, this link is an example of how a multiplicity of similar sources can frustrate any attempt to name a specific source as the root of, in this case, a character.

Although Shakespeare mentions 'Ephesians' twice in relation to Falstaff, in *Henry IV Part II* and *The Merry Wives of Windsor*, the ideas of wickedness and the need for personal reform that he applies to the character are commonplace throughout the Old and New Testaments, and also in the moral teachings of the pagan Greeks and Romans. In Book II of the Greek writer Xenophon's reminiscences of the philosopher Socrates, Socrates tries to persuade the dissolute Aristippus to exercise 'self-control in the matters of eating, drinking, sleeping, and the cravings of lust'. It is likely that Shakespeare knew, or knew of, this dialogue because, as we shall see, it includes a story about the god Hercules which may relate to the playwright's conception of the character of Mark Antony in *Antony and Cleopatra*.

If we accept the link between Falstaff and Ephesians, we cannot, however, assume that

Shakespeare read Ephesians for himself, then recalled the Epistle when he came to write the Henry IV plays and *The Merry Wives of Windsor*. He may have heard the Epistle, or part of it, read out in church, or heard a sermon on it. If it is true that he owned and read a strange little book like Lambarde's *Archaionomia,* he may also have read some book of Biblical commentaries, one of which addressed the Epistle to the Ephesians.

Even if Shakespeare read Ephesians directly, the question of which version he read is not easy to resolve.

With the 'small Latin and less Greek' that his fellow-playwright Ben Jonson insisted that he had, Shakespeare may have been able to tackle the original Greek of the New Testament, or read it in the so-called 'Vulgate' Latin version. As for English translations, the famous King James Version came out in 1611, around the time Shakespeare is thought to have finished his career as a playwright. The Biblical extracts in the paragraphs above are from the Geneva Bible (1587), but Shakespeare may also have used the Bishop's Bible (1568) and the Roman Catholic Douay-Rheims Bible (New Testament published 1582). Although, as their names suggest, two of these Bible translations were first published in continental Europe, they are all in the English language.

Focussing on the 'old man' passage (Ephesians IV, 22) which King James renders as 'put off concerning the former conversation the old man, which is corrupt according to the deceitful lusts,' there is little to choose between the Bishop's Bible, Geneva and Douay-Rheims:

Bishop's Bible:

' . . . lay down, according to the former conversation, the old man, which is corrupt, according to the lusts of error.'

Douay-Rheims:

' . . . put off, according to former conversation, the old man, who is corrupted according to the desire of error.'

Geneva:

' . . . cast off, concerning the conversation in time past, that old man, which is corrupt through the deceivable lusts.'

In the same way that Shakespeare may have gained his knowledge of the Bible from a number of sources, he also seems to have drawn his information about English history from a multiplicity of sources. As we shall see, many of the ideas used in *Richard III* originally came from Sir Thomas More's *History* of that monarch, but in those days before copyright, More's words were recycled verbatim by later chroniclers.

Although it is sometimes hard to link Shakespeare plays to sources with complete confidence, it is still worthwhile to try to trace where the playwright got his ideas. Comparing sources and plays is something like viewing a series of photographs taken during the making of a statue: the first picture being, perhaps, of the stone being cut out of a cliff in the quarry, and the last being a picture of the finished work. Such a sequence of pictures can give us insights into how the finished product was made. We can see the creative decisions Shakespeare made while turning his sources into effective drama, and we are sometimes surprised by choices that seem to go against the grain of the originals. In *Richard II*, for instance, the playwright shows Richard's queen as a grown woman, whereas historically she was a small child when her royal husband died. And as we shall see, whereas in the strange little scene in *Antony and Cleopatra* where Cleopatra's guards hear the god Hercules leaving Antony, in Plutarch's original the god in question is Bacchus.

Shakespeare made a puzzling, not to say controversial choice with the character of Juliet in his *Romeo and Juliet.* In two of his sources for this play, Juliet is sixteen and eighteen respectively. In Shakespeare's play, she is thirteen. The whole action of *Romeo and Juliet* takes place over just a few days, whereas in one of the sources, Arthur Brooke's poem *The Tragical History of Romeus and Juliet* (1562), the lovers are married for a month or more before their story turns tragic.

As with his compression of the action of the story of *Romeo and Juliet*, the choices Shakespeare makes in handling his sources sometimes draw attention to the practicalities of the theatres of his period. He had to write plays that lasted just a few hours, which could be performed by a cast of about twenty. Although Shakespeare wrote many female parts, these would have been played not by women but by men. Younger women or girls, such as Juliet in *Romeo and Juliet*, would be played by young boys. One reason why the playwright made his Juliet thirteen years old may have been because the only boy who could play the part couldn't look any older. Shakespeare's plays also had to have enough action in them to hold the attention of an audience made up partly of people with relatively little education, some of whom may have been quite illiterate.

The playwright also had to face political and religious constraints, as well as practical ones. If a play was seen to be seditious (if, for instance, it seemed to criticise the ruling dynasty) this could lead to endless trouble for the playwright and his company: they could end up in prison, or even hanged. And the theatre of Elizabethan and Jacobean times was not allowed to enact any Christian religious services on stage: no weddings, baptisms or coronations, for example.

An awareness of the practicalities of the theatre of Shakespeare's time can inform modern productions of the plays; as can a knowledge of their sources. A director who finds out from Plutarch that Mark Antony deliberately dressed so as to look like the Roman god Hercules, for instance, could use this information to inform choices by his costume designer and the actor who plays Antony himself. Likewise a knowledge of Thomas More's account of the restless body-language of Richard III could add an extra dimension to an actor's performance.

Too close a concentration on the sources could, however, distort a production in an unproductive way. After reading about the historical and colonial aspect of *The Tempest*, a director might think the character of Caliban should be played as a member of one of the Tupí tribes of what is now Brazil. But this would be to ignore important aspects of Caliban's character and back-story: he is, after all, supposed to be a creature conceived by the devil with an Algerian witch.

As well as informing modern productions, and our response to older productions preserved on film or video, research into Shakespeare's sources can put the investigator in touch with the rich cultural milieu of Shakespeare's time, and also with some important works of literature from that and earlier generations.

On the other hand, some texts that are acknowledged as *bona fide* sources of Shakespeare could never be classified as great literature. These include wordy, static plays such as those on the subject of Antony and Cleopatra by Mary Herbert and her accomplice Samuel Daniel; also biased, repetitive chronicles; frothy, interminable prose romances; and dreary, moralising and sycophantic poems.

Some of Shakespeare's sources are indeed base metal, and they remind us how Shakespeare's talent for transformation resembles the supposed transformative skills of the alchemists. Many of these rusty works are now remembered mainly because Shakespeare made use of them, but have little in themselves to recommend them to modern readers.

Shakespeare's use of earlier literature, whatever its quality, somewhat diminishes his claim to be an 'original' writer; but it is likely that this would not have bothered him or his contemporaries. Originality was not much valued in those days: like Chaucer and his generation, Shakespeare's contemporaries liked to stay connected to older traditions of literature, and to claim authority from those traditions. If he wrote the following lines in *Pericles Prince of Tyre*, the text of which has come down to us in a rather mangled form, then Shakespeare was referencing the reliance of Chaucer's generation on their sources. The lines are spoken near the start of the play by Chaucer's friend the poet John Gower, who acts as the chorus or narrator in *Pericles*:

This Antioch, then: Antiochus the Great
Built up this city, for his chiefest seat:
The fairest in all Syria,
I tell you what mine authors say

Although he embraced the authors who had gone before him, Shakespeare was also keen to reflect his own age, and the stage conventions of the time seem to have required, for instance, that plays set in ancient Rome be staged in something like what to Shakespeare's audience would have been modern dress. In *Coriolanus*, for example, people throw their caps in the air to express delight; Cleopatra demands that her servant Charmian cut her lace (to loosen her corset); and artillery is mentioned in *Macbeth*, at least two centuries before it was first used in Europe.

A sort of manifesto for this kind of writing – reflecting the present – is spoken by Hamlet in Act III scene 2 of his play. He tells us about 'the purpose of playing':

whose end, both at the first and now, was and is, to hold, as 'twere, the mirror up to nature; to show virtue her own feature, scorn her own image, and the very age and body of the time his form and pressure.

Hamlet's words here apply to theatre in general, but in the context of this scene they refer directly to a play called *The Murder of Gonzago*, based on a text which Hamlet tells us is 'extant, and writ in choice Italian'. We have already met with the other play mentioned in *Hamlet;* an unnamed piece evidently based on the ancient story of the fall of Troy. Both of these plays seem to have been made up by Shakespeare to feature in *Hamlet*: it is unlikely that either of them existed in their entirety in any form. From the 'Troy play', Hamlet himself recites from memory the speech beginning with these lines:

The rugged Pyrrhus, he whose sable arms,
Black as his purpose, did the night resemble
When he lay couched in the ominous horse,
Hath now his dread and black complexion smear'd
With heraldry more dismal; head to foot
Now is he total gules; horridly trick'd

With blood of fathers, mothers, daughters, sons,
Baked and impasted with the parching streets,
That lend a tyrannous and damned light
To their lord's murder: roasted in wrath and fire,
And thus o'er-sized with coagulate gore,
With eyes like carbuncles, the hellish Pyrrhus
Old grandsire Priam seeks.

Although Hamlet's advice to the players, advising them, in effect, to make their work relevant to the here and now, is surely right, the prince's fondness for this doomed 'Troy play' suggests that Hamlet's taste in plays is that of a scholar, and not a man of the people. Although he claims that the play is 'excellent' and written with 'modesty', it would seem, from the speech begun by Hamlet and completed by the First Player, that it is horribly over-written. The speech remembered by Hamlet and the First Player is also 'too long', as Polonius remarks; although when the old man says this, the speech still has another thirteen and a half lines to go. If the speech is supposed to be from a play, who is supposed to be speaking it, and in what dramatic context, if any?

The clearest source for this speech is a section of book two of Virgil's *Aeneid*, where Aeneas himself describes the sack of

Troy:

> ... For Pyrrhus, red with Priam's blood, is hard at hand, who slays
> The son before the father's face, the father slays upon
> The altar. Holy Mother, then, for this thou ledst me on
> Through fire and sword! - that I might see our house filled with the foe,
> My father old, Ascanius, Creusa lying low,
> All weltering in each other's blood, and murdered wretchedly.

(Trans. William Morris, 1876, Bk II, 662-7)

But this is part of a long speech from a narrative poem, not a play. In his play *Troilus and Cressida*, also based on the Trojan war, Shakespeare *dramatises* scenes like this, rather than having them described at length by some sort of chorus, or a character recounting past action.

In the 'Pyrrhus' speech Shakespeare may be commenting on the lumbering, pedantic drama of an earlier generation, which was so besotted with sources such as Homer's *Iliad*, Virgil's *Aeneid* and the drama of ancient Greece and Rome that it included much static speechifying and too little actual drama. Such plays as *Gorboduc* by Thomas Norton and Thomas Sackville (1561), the first English play in blank verse, seem to have been part of an unsuccessful attempt to bring the stiff, formal style of the plays of the Roman philosopher Seneca into English drama. The imaginary 'Troy play', which Hamlet loves so much, may be Shakespeare's comment on how *not* to use certain kinds of sources.

Troilus and Cressida, the 'Troy play', *The Tempest* and parts of many other works suggest that Shakespeare was familiar with the legends surrounding the Trojan war; and indeed it is unlikely that a literate man of his generation in England could *not* have been acquainted with them. Shakespeare probably read Virgil and Homer, if only in English translations such as those of Thomas Twyne (Virgil) and George Chapman (Homer). But what else did he read?

In his verse preface to what we call the First Folio of 1623 (an early attempt to publish all of Shakespeare's plays) his fellow-playwright Ben Jonson asserted, as we know, that the man from Stratford had 'small Latin and less Greek'; but Shakespeare's plays and poems seem to suggest that he had a good knowledge of

Greek and Latin classics beyond Virgil and Homer, as well as works in French, Italian and other languages. It seems that he had on his shelves, if only temporarily, a lot of English translations of foreign-language works, both ancient and modern. Among these translations were some of the finest ever made in English, including John Florio's translation of the French philosopher Montaigne's *Essays*, translations of the Roman poet Ovid by Arthur Golding, and of the Greek historian Plutarch by Thomas North.

Shakespeare's was a good time for translations, as it was for original poetry and drama. As to older English poetry, we know that Shakespeare knew and used the fourteenth-century master Geoffrey Chaucer, and Chaucer's contemporary John Gower, who, as we have seen, even features as a character in *Pericles*.

Part of the reason why translations were so celebrated by Shakespeare's contemporaries has to do with their aforementioned respect for tradition, and their disregard for what we would call originality. Writers like George Chapman, the translator of Homer, whom Shakespeare may have referred to in several of his sonnets, were highly respected for their translations, a fact which no doubt encouraged other writers to make contributions in this field.

Although the practice might make Shakespeare seem old-fashioned and unoriginal, in borrowing his stories from earlier authors he was doing what many playwrights and screen-writers continue to do in the twenty-first century. Of the top ten most profitable English-language feature films released in 2014, for instance, only one of them (*The Lego Movie*) has any claim to have an original story, and even that includes the cartoon character Batman, who first appeared in a comic-book in 1939. Of the remaining nine top films of 2014, no less than five are based on comic-books, two are based on novels and one on an autobiography.

One advantage of re-using old material is that if the play or film has a familiar-sounding name, potential audiences may be more willing to pay to see it than they might a completely original work. Hence Hollywood's many sequels and re-makes, Shakespeare's historical plays in long series, and his plays based on subjects already handled by earlier poets, translators or playwrights. The playwright not only recycled old material originated by others: he also re-used his own best ideas: Falstaff, one of Shakespeare's most popular characters, appears in no less than three plays, and there is a long speech and much conversation about him in a fourth.

When he wasn't reading older literature, either in the original or in translation, Shakespeare was either reading, watching, acting in or even co-authoring plays by his contemporaries. As an intelligent actor, a playwright and a share-holder in a theatre, he seems to have developed a keen eye for what worked on stage, what would work for the actors he was writing for, what could be appropriated, what could be improved on, and what should be avoided.

Shakespeare's use of his contemporaries' plays seems to have caused some resentment, particularly in the heart of one Robert Greene, who wrote the following in his *Greene's Groatsworth of Wit* (1592):

. . . there is an upstart crow, beautified with our feathers, that with his 'tiger's heart wrapped in a player's hide', supposes he is as well able to bombast out a blank verse as the best of you: and being an absolute Johannes factotum, is in his own conceit the only Shake-scene in a country.

'Tiger's heart wrapped in a player's hide' is Greene's parody of a line from Act I, scene 4 of Shakespeare's *Henry VI Part III*, where Richard, Duke of York implies that Queen Margaret has a 'tiger's heart, wrapped in a woman's hide'. Greene's phrase 'beautified with our feathers' would seem to suggest some sort of plagiarism on Shakespeare's part, but it may also suggest the mediocre Greene's frustration that this Warwickshire 'upstart' has turned the conventions of the Elizabethan drama, including blank verse, into such effective plays.

Robert Greene was one of the 'University Wits', a group christened by George Saintsbury in his 1887 *History of Elizabethan Literature*. The leading member of this group, who far exceeded Greene in the quality of his output, was Christopher Marlowe, who was born in 1564, the same year as Shakespeare, and whose work had a profound effect on the Stratford man.

Saintsbury identified some characteristics shared by the plays of the University Wits, a group that included not only Greene and Marlowe but also Thomas Lodge, Thomas Nashe, John Lyly and George Peele.

According to Saintsbury, there was generally too much 'bombast' in their plays, a word Greene uses in his comment on Shakespeare the 'upstart crow', and which refers to an over-stuffed, over-elaborate style. The author of the *History of Elizabethan Literature* also complains of the faulty structure of the plays of the University Wits, the long ranting speeches of some of their characters, and what he calls their 'foible of classical allusion':

The heathen gods and goddesses, the localities of Greek and Roman poetry, even the more out-of-the-way commonplaces of classical literature, are put in the mouths of all the characters without the remotest attempt to consider propriety or relevance.

According to Saintsbury, part of Shakespeare's achievement was in creating more effective dramatic structures, banishing rant and bombast, and restricting classical allusion according to 'propriety' and 'relevance'. This is surely right, and we can see that his treatment of the sources of his poetic elaborations was part of the story of his creative success. Saintsbury identifies Shakespeare as the leader of a group of playwrights who were also actors, or otherwise involved with the theatres of the time, and were concerned more with what happened on stage than how plays reflected the lengthy and expensive educations of their authors.

As a man of the theatre, Shakespeare could hardly have avoided having a good knowledge of his contemporary English-language playwrights and their works. What is more surprising is his knowledge of the popular Italian dramatic form, the Commedia dell'arte, or Comedy of Skills. As we shall see in the context of *The Tempest*, he may have been able to follow Commedia performances to the point where he was tempted to appropriate elements of their plots. He seems also to have had a knowledge of the stock characters of the Commedia, including Pantalone ('the lean and slipper'd pantaloon' of *As You Like It* Act II scene 7) and the bragging Spanish soldier (Don Armado in *Love's Labours Lost*). Whether Shakespeare saw these semi-improvised plays when Commedia troupes toured to England, or on a trip to the Continent (for which we have no direct evidence) is impossible to say.

As well as translations, poems and plays, Shakespeare seems to have read or otherwise known the equivalents in his time of newspapers and magazines. These were often sensational reports of recent events, published in pamphlet form. He also read history, in the form of the chronicle books that were published in his day. Of the authors of these, one whose name will be forever linked with Shakespeare's is Raphael Holinshed.

It should not be imagined that the following book is an attempt to cover the subject of Shakespeare's sources exhaustively, even for the three plays that are examined in detail: *Richard III*, *The Tempest* and *Antony and Cleopatra*. These plays have been chosen partly because Shakespeare stuck remarkably close to his sources in parts of all three of them, and partly because the range of sources, Shakespeare's use of them in these plays, and the sources themselves, are particularly interesting.

The three include an English history play and one based on ancient Roman history, and these represent two important areas of the playwright's background reading. Some of the sources used for *Richard III* were also used for other history plays, and the sources of *Antony and Cleopatra* served Shakespeare for Roman plays such as *Coriolanus* and *Julius Caesar*. *The Tempest* is intriguing as it does not seem to have an obvious direct source, and investigators have been forced to point to various possible sources of aspects of the play.

II. Richard III

Thomas More's *History of King Richard III*; Hall's Chronicle and Holinshed's Chronicle

King Richard III, who reigned for just two years from 1483 to 1485, is of special interest to twenty-first century readers because his body was discovered under a car-park in the English city of Leicester in 2012. When DNA and other evidence confirmed that the Leicester body really was Richard's, and that the king had indeed been a hunchback, researchers knew that they were analysing the remains not only of a famous (or notorious) king, but also the real-life original of an important Shakespearian character.

The body was found partly because of the efforts of Ricardians – people who believe that Richard has been maligned for hundreds of years, and that he was actually a good king, and not a murderous tyrant. Ricardians, like the Baconians who believe that Shakespeare didn't write the plays attributed to him, are to be found all over the world.

Shakespeare is sometimes blamed for depicting Richard as a monster, but the playwright inherited the then current view of the last Plantagenet king from his sources. These sources are thought to include a chronicle book called *The Union of the Two Noble and Illustrious Families of Lancaster and York*, usually referred to as Hall's Chronicle, which was written by Edward Hall and first published in 1548. For his plays about English history, Shakespeare often used a similar book called *Holinshed's Chronicle* (1577), and for *Richard III* he seems to have had both Hall and Holinshed to hand.

The full title of Hall's book is a clue to the stance the chronicler took in its pages. He was using his chronicle to celebrate the 'union of the two noble and illustrious families of Lancaster and York', which means he was celebrating the birth of the Tudor dynasty, which began when Henry VII became king. The 'union' part refers to the fact that Henry, whose surname was 'Tudor', but who was derived from the Lancaster dynasty, married Elizabeth *of York* soon after he ascended the throne. He first wore the crown after he had won the battle of Bosworth near Leicester: the same battle at which Richard III was killed.

By the time Hall's Chronicle was first published, the Tudor dynasty had been in power for over sixty years: Hall wrote his Chronicle, and Shakespeare wrote *Richard III*, during the reign of Elizabeth I, the granddaughter of Henry VII.

Despite the longevity of the Tudor dynasty (altogether it lasted for well over a century, and only ended when Elizabeth died in 1603) it was plain to anyone who could understand a family tree that the Tudor claim to the throne was tenuous at best. They claimed it through the second husband of the widow of King Henry V; but doubts about the claims of the Lancastrian dynasty went back to a time well before the name Tudor was added to the mix. Henry V inherited the crown from his father Henry IV, but *he* was a usurper, who took the crown from Richard II and then oversaw the death of that earlier Richard.

The unfortunate King Richard II had himself inherited the crown, as a child of ten, from his grandfather Edward III (his father, Edward the Black Prince, had died earlier). The usurper Henry Bolingbroke, who became Henry IV, could only claim the crown via John of Gaunt, the fourth son of Edward III. Richard III claimed the crown through the third son, Lionel Duke of Clarence.

Arguments over who had the right to reign were among the causes of what we now call the Wars of the Roses, wars fought sporadically between the houses of Lancaster and York over a period of some thirty years. These wars were 'covered' by Shakespeare in four of his history plays – the three Henry VI plays, and *Richard III*. The playwright later turned to an earlier part of this story in his plays *Richard II*, *Henry IV Parts I and II*, and *Henry V*.

The rickety nature of the Tudor claim to the throne is one reason why chroniclers working under that dynasty were careful to make Richard III appear a bad king. The Tudor position was that he might have had a better claim to the throne, but that he was evil, so it was right for the Lancastrian side to reassert itself under the Tudor name, and wipe him out.

In modern terms, the Tudors, and the chroniclers who wrote under them, were protecting the royal 'brand'; and they certainly didn't want anyone hankering after the old brand that theirs had replaced. In fact the comparison with modern consumer brands is very apposite: the Tudors even had their own logo: the Tudor rose with its red and white petals. Richard III's logo was rather sterner: a white boar.

Edward Hall, an English lawyer, MP and old Etonian who died in the year before his chronicle was published, made use of an earlier account of Richard III written by Thomas More, the famous 'man for all seasons' portrayed by Paul Schofield in the film based on Robert Bolt's play. More was Lord Chancellor to, and ultimately a victim of, King Henry VIII, and was declared a saint by the Roman Catholic Church in 1935.

More seems to have written his *History of King Richard III* (around 1515) because he had inside information on the events of that reign from his old master, John Morton, archbishop of Canterbury, who had been bishop of Ely when Richard III seized the throne.

Morton, who is a named character in Shakespeare's play of Richard III, had been present at many of the events recounted by both Thomas More and Shakespeare, and had used his powers of persuasion to set the duke of Buckingham against the king, and thus provoke the rebellion that led to Richard's death at Bosworth.

Unrestricted by copyright laws, which didn't exist as such in his day, Edward Hall pretty much copied out large sections of More's *History*, mixing in information from other sources, clarifying things, moving some sections around, and deleting others. By the same token, Holinshed made extensive use of Hall.

One example of a clarification provided by Hall in his text, which is much longer than More's, relates to the attempts to marry the bachelor King Edward IV to a continental princess. More tells us that this princess was Spanish, whereas Shakespeare insists she was a lady called Bona of Savoy. Hall clears up the confusion by explaining that a Spanish princess *had* been in the running, but was ultimately rejected as being too young:

. . . who so will diligently consider, and in equal

balance ponder, the youth and appetite of King Edward, and the tender age and minority of this noble damosel, may evidently perceive, that it was neither decent nor convenient, for him nor his realm, to expect and tarry the maturity and full age of this noble princess, nor that he being a prince, well cherished, of lusty courage, and apt to generation, would or could live sole and unmarried without a wife, till she were of age, meet and convenient for his bed.

According to Hall, the next candidate was indeed Bona, but this match had to be aborted because it was revealed that Edward had already married an Englishwoman, Elizabeth Woodville. Hall and Thomas More tell the tale of Edward's controversial marriage in lengthy flash-backs: Shakespeare sets out the story in his play *Henry VI Part I*, but the issue is still a live one in *Richard III*: Richard and his co-conspirator the duke of Buckingham try to cast doubt on the legitimacy of Edward's ill-fated sons, the princes in the Tower, by suggesting that their brother's marriage to Elizabeth Woodville was not itself legitimate. Wasn't he promised to Lady Bona, and even to another English Elizabeth, Elizabeth Lucy?

RICHARD
Touched you the bastardy of Edward's children?

BUCKINGHAM
I did; with his contract with Lady Lucy
And his contract by deputy in France

(*Richard III*, Act III scene 7)

Hall's additions to More's *History* appear throughout his version; but he seems to have felt obliged to add a lot at the end because the man for all seasons had left the story unfinished. More broke off in the middle of the beginning of Buckingham's conspiracy, by which time Richard was already king, and had killed the princes in the Tower. A lot of the content Hall added is surprisingly sympathetic to Richard, although he makes it clear that the murders of the princes, and other crimes committed by him, marked him indelibly as an evil tyrant.

Hall explains away the good deeds of King Richard as attempts to win favour with the people and atone for his crimes:

. . . he showed himself more just, more meeker, more familiar, more liberal (especially amongst the poor people) than before he had accustomed to do . . . He furthermore began and enterprised divers things as well public as private . . . he began to found a college of a hundred priests, which foundation with the founder shortly took an end. To please the common people also, he in his high court of parliament enacted divers and sundry good laws and profitable statutes . . .

Even King Richard's worthwhile treaty with the Scots, which Hall sets out in great detail, is, according to Hall, a product of the king's guilt and fear:

King Richard being thus tormented and tossed in his own conceit and imagination, called to his remembrance that considerations amities, and other honest bonds and pacts, made, concluded and appointed between princes and politic governors are the cause efficient and special introduction that their realms and countries are fortified and munited [strengthened] with a double power, that is to say, with their own strength and the aid of their friends, devised with himself to practise a league and amity with the king of Scots.

Neither Shakespeare nor Thomas More give us these details about Richard's good deeds, but the play and its sources are agreed that the king was 'tormented and tossed in his own conceit and imagination'; secretly racked with guilt and fearful of retribution.

In Shakespeare and his sources, nightmares are a symptom of Richard's emotional agony. These terrifying dreams revisit him the night before the battle of Bosworth, and here Shakespeare turns a brief mention from Hall and Holinshed into an elaborate scene in which both Richard and his opponent the earl of Richmond dream about the same people – most of them victims of Richard. Whereas these ghosts have encouraging words for Richmond, they tell Richard to 'despair and die'.

These recognisable spirits replace the 'divers images like terrible devils' that visit Richard in Holinshed's account, and they serve to add a creepy atmosphere to the last hours of Richard as depicted in the play. They also help to remind us of Richard's crimes committed not only in the course of *Richard III* but also in the Henry VI plays; and the ghosts' support for Richmond, that 'quiet untroubled soul', reinforces both his claim to the throne and the play's final note of the victory of good over evil.

Richard's psychological torments make

him a more sympathetic, or at least a more human, character, but from the point of view of the Christianity of sixteenth-century England, his consciousness of his own sins must have made him seem more guilty. When, in the play, he suffers a sort of 'dark night of the soul' after waking from his nightmare, he is horribly conscious of his own guilt, yet he still spurs himself on to more wicked deeds:

By the apostle Paul, shadows to-night
Have struck more terror to the soul of Richard
Than can the substance of ten thousand soldiers
Armed in proof, and led by shallow Richmond.
It is not yet near day. Come, go with me;
Under our tents I'll play the eaves-dropper,
To see if any mean to shrink from me.

(V, 2)

A feature of Richard about which Shakespeare and his sources are in agreement is the deformity of his body. The most striking difference between Shakespeare's treatment of this, and that of Holinshed and Hall, is the *placement* of the details of Richard's deformity within their respective narratives. Holinshed, following

Hall, tells us practically the whole story of Richard's rise and fall before he gets around to describing his physical appearance, some fifty pages into his account of Richard's reign. By contrast, Shakespeare has Richard enter right at the beginning of his play; and it takes the future king only thirteen blank verse lines of his introductory speech to mention his deformity. By then, it is obvious to any sighted person in the audience who has a reasonable view of the stage that Richard is indeed deformed, unless the actor in question is playing down Richard's physical abnormalities. Anyone watching the play as the culmination of some ambitious plan to present Shakespeare's *Richard III* and the three Henry VI plays all together will already have heard Richard's detailed description of his person in Act III scene 2 of *Henry VI part III*:

Why, love forswore me in my mother's womb:
And, for I should not deal in her soft laws,
She did corrupt frail nature with some bribe,
To shrink mine arm up like a wither'd shrub;
To make an envious mountain on my back,
Where sits deformity to mock my body;
To shape my legs of an unequal size;
To disproportion me in every part,
Like to a chaos, or an unlick'd bear-whelp

That carries no impression like the dam.

Readers familiar with Laurence Olivier's 1955 film of *Richard III* may recognise these lines, even if they don't know the Henry VI plays: Olivier transplanted them into his screenplay.

Actors assaying the part of Richard tend to give us the whole panoply of deformities as described in *Henry VI part 3*; but More, Hall and Holinshed are more restrained in their accounts of Richard's shape, giving him only unequal shoulders and a withered arm. And whereas Shakespeare tells us that Richard's shape is the *cause* of his wickedness, Hall and Holinshed, when they describe him, put his shape *together with* his warped personality, but don't really say that the one is the cause of the other. Both are more interested in Richard's wicked personality and his restless physical presence, which, together with his 'timorous dreams', they take to be symptoms of his wicked nature. Here is Thomas More:

When he stood musing, he would bite and chew busily his nether lip; as who said, that his fierce nature in his cruel body always chafed, stirred, and was ever unquiet. Beside that, the dagger which he wore, he would (when he studied) with his hand pluck up and down in the sheath to the midst, never drawing it fully out.

I have argued elsewhere* that Richard's physical restlessness may have been a symptom of the constant pain he would have suffered from the arthritis in his back. Experts found signs of both arthritis and scoliosis (curvature of the spine) in the body of Richard III that was discovered in Leicester in 2012.

In a way that would seem to pre-empt Freud's analysis of human motivation, Shakespeare tells us that Richard is 'determined to prove a villain' because his body makes him unsuited to capering 'nimbly in a lady's chamber'. In both plays, Richard himself tells us this, but in typical Shakespearian fashion, the playwright undermines Richard's assertion by having the king get rid of his wife Lady Anne in order to follow the scheme of marrying his niece, Elizabeth (later queen to Henry IV). Even when he can sleep in 'a lady's chamber' every night, his ambition and his appetite for mischief continue unabated.

*See my edition of *The History of King Richard III* by Thomas More, Langley Press, 2015

Modern readers and playgoers, coming from a society that tries to discourage negative attitudes to disabled people, are sometimes uneasy about Shakespeare's explicit link between bodily deformity and personal wickedness: this link is not so explicit in the sources. Indeed, Hall and Holinshed remind us that Richard had at least some good qualities, and that his infamous reputation need not have developed at all. Here is Holinshed:

> . . . if he had continued still protector, and suffered his nephews to have lived and reigned, no doubt but the realm had prospered, and he as much praised and loved as he is now had in hatred . . .

The 'Formal Vice'

Shakespeare is good enough to tell us about one of his sources for *Richard III:* in this case a source for some aspects of Richard's personality.

In Act III scene 1 Richard, who is still only duke of Gloucester at this time, breaks off from an ominous discussion with the uncrowned child-king, Edward V, to speak to the audience in an aside, in which he compares himself to 'the formal Vice, Iniquity'. Richard is referring to a character called Iniquity, a personification of that particular vice, such as might have appeared in one of the so-called miracle plays of medieval England, or in a Tudor interlude – a type of short play that was sometimes presented as part of the entertainment at banquets organised by the aristocracy and other magnates.

There are two extant Tudor interludes that feature a character called Iniquity; one called *Nice Wanton* (1560) and the second *King Darius*. In *Darius*, described on its 1577 title page as 'both pithy and pleasant', Iniquity comes on straight after the Prologue and speaks directly to the audience, making it clear that he intends mischief:

How now my masters, how goeth the world now?
I came gladly to talk with you.
But soft, is there nobody here,
Truly, I do not like this gear.
I thought I should have found somebody,
Let me look better yet I pray ye.
I am mad now, to the sole of my foot,

An they were here, I would lay them on the coat
Ah, whoreson knaves have you thus me mocked,
Surely I will break their head,
Come no near it were for you best,
If you do, it shall be for your unrest.

The 'formal Vice' was a feature of two types of English drama that preceded the Elizabethan theatre and the plays of Shakespeare, but personifications also feature as characters in Shakespeare's plays, and in the elaborate masques of the seventeenth century. A character called Rumour appears 'in a skin coat full of winged tongues' in Thomas Campion's *Masque of Squires* (1613) and in the second part of Shakespeare's *Henry IV* Rumour appears 'painted full of tongues'. Shakespeare also has a personification of Time in his *Winter's Tale*.

The Jew of Malta by Christopher Marlowe

As the Elizabethan drama gained in sophistication and realism, it was natural for the 'formal Vice' to be replaced by 'real' characters, who were not personifications of vices, virtues or other concepts. In *The Jew of Malta*, a play written in 1589 or 1590 by Shakespeare's contemporary Christopher Marlowe, Barabas, the eponymous Jew, regularly speaks directly to the audience in soliloquys and asides, updating them on the wicked plans he is designing and putting into action against the Christians of Malta:

They hop'd my daughter would ha' been a nun;
But she's at home, and I have bought a house
As great and fair as is the governor's:
And there, in spite of Malta, will I dwell,
Having Ferneze's hand; whose heart I'll have,
Ay, and his son's too, or it shall go hard.

Marlowe's *Jew of Malta* may seem a more natural source for Shakespeare's *Merchant of Venice* than for his *Richard III*, but Barabas's role as both narrator and instigator of the action, anti-hero and villain, makes him an interesting parallel with Richard Plantagenet. Like several of Marlowe's heroes, Barabas is ambitious and overreaching, and it may be that, having seen the electrifying effect these characters had on Marlowe's audiences, Shakespeare wanted to experiment with such a character when he took up his pen to write *Richard III*. Other wicked narrator anti-heroes in Shakespeare include Iago in *Othello*, who narrates the action as he steers it along its dark path, and has almost as many lines as Richard has in *Richard III*.

Richard III follows as the next play after the three parts of Shakespeare's *Henry VI*, and it is possible to discern, in those three earlier plays, Shakespeare's approach becoming more sophisticated and theatrical, as the actor/writer gains experience of writing, performing and watching his own work. One of the things that makes *Richard III* stand out from the *Henry VI* plays is the title-character's dominance, something which contrasts with the earlier plays, which have a plethora of characters, none of whom predominate as much as Richard does in *Richard III*. Even King Henry VI himself doesn't stand out much in these earlier plays, but then that reflects the chaotic political situation Shakespeare is trying to portray.

As well as the sources described above, in writing *Richard III* Shakespeare also seems to have made use of a book of poems called *A Mirror for Magistrates*, an anonymous play called *The True History of Richard III*, a translation of Seneca's *Hercules Furens*, and some other texts.

It should be remembered that in *Richard III* Shakespeare was dramatising events that had happened only one hundred and fifty years earlier, much as we today (in 2017) might write about events that took place in 1907. It is possible that he was able to benefit from stories told at second or third hand, particularly by Londoners whose grandparents or great-grandparents, for instance, might have witnessed some of the events he put into his play. Such sources or 'living histories' are usually impossible to identify.

III. The Tempest

The Tempest, which is usually taken to be one of Shakespeare's latest plays (if not his last) is interesting from the point of view of its sources, because there seems to be no known surviving source that accounts for its story.

The narrative of the play combines diverse elements, which can be classified under two headings: politics and magic. Running alongside the tale of spirits and spells is the story of how Prospero, described in the *dramatis personae* of the play as 'the right duke of Milan' sets himself up to return from exile and regain his dukedom.

Prospero is stranded with his daughter Miranda on an island which, logic would seem to dictate, must be somewhere in the Mediterranean, since some characters who are shipwrecked there were travelling between Tunis in North Africa, and Italy.

'By providence divine,' some of the very men who conspired to exile Prospero are among those shipwrecked, and the exiled duke sets about punishing them for their transgression, though without killing anyone.

Prospero is able to use magic to turn the whole island against his enemies, including its spirits, led by the enigmatic Ariel. Prospero's command of the island is founded on his own magical powers, which are derived from certain books he was able to take with him when he and Miranda were cast adrift in the sea, in:

A rotten carcass of a butt, not rigged,
Nor tackle, sail, nor mast. The very rats
Instinctively had quit it.

As his name suggests, Ariel is a spirit of the air: Prospero refers to him as 'thou, which art but air' (V, 1). As such, Ariel cannot be fully understood as a character without a grasp of Jacobean science, which insisted that everything in nature was composed of a combination of what were called the four elements: fire, air, earth and water. This doctrine appears regularly throughout Shakespeare, and perhaps reaches its most sublime application in *Antony and*

Cleopatra, when the Egyptian queen, on the verge of her suicide, declares:

I am fire and air; my other elements
I give to baser life.

(V, 2)

Ariel's counterpart in *The Tempest* is Caliban, 'a savage and deformed slave', whose name is an anagram of 'cannibal' (bearing in mind that Jacobean spelling was very flexible), and whom Prospero refers to as 'earth' and 'filth'.

Critics, artists, theatre directors, film and television producers, actors and designers have long struggled with Caliban, not knowing quite what to make of him. In the late twentieth and early twenty-first century, when the West is finally facing up to the historical atrocities committed in the name of colonialism, Caliban has become, in some minds, an archetypal 'native', oppressed by the 'pale, male' colonial power, Prospero.

Montaigne, Florio and Strachey

Reservations about colonialism were expressed in Europe not just after, but during and right at the beginning of European colonialism as a historical phenomenon.

One of the first to express misgivings about what was happening to the natives of 'newly-discovered' lands was the French philosopher Michel de Montaigne (1533-1592).

The book that has secured Montaigne's immortality is his *Essays*, published in 1580, and released in an English translation in 1603, seven or more years before Shakespeare is thought to have written *The Tempest*.

The *Essays* cover a bewildering range of subjects, from Greek philosophers, to the education of children, and the sense of smell. The essay most relevant to Shakespeare's *Tempest* is called *On Cannibals*, though others, including one on a deformed child and another on the custom of wearing clothes, may have influenced Shakespeare's play.

Although Shakespeare didn't know Montaigne personally, he may have known the translator of the 1603 English version of the *Essays*: in fact it is highly unlikely that he *didn't* know him quite well.

The translator was John Florio (1553-1625) who was born in London but had at least one Italian parent. His father, Michelangelo Florio, had come to England to escape persecution as a Protestant, but the family had to decamp to Switzerland during the reign of Mary, the Catholic queen of England. John returned during the reign of Elizabeth I.

Apart from Shakespeare's use of Florio's Montaigne in *The Tempest*, another link between the playwright and Florio, the self-styled 'Englishman in Italiane', was Henry Wriothesley, third earl of Southampton (1573-1624). Florio worked as Southampton's tutor; and Shakespeare had dedicated his narrative poems *Venus and Adonis* and *The Rape of Lucrece* to the earl.

Some say the relationship between Shakespeare and Southampton went deeper than just that between a writer and his aristocratic patron. It is possible that the mysterious 'Mr W.H.' to whom Shakespeare's sonnets are dedicated is none other than Southampton; that he features as the 'fair youth' mentioned in the sonnets, and that he and Shakespeare might even have been lovers.

Florio, the earl's personal 'renaissance man', had received an impressive Continental education, and it is tempting to think of he and Shakespeare enthusiastically discussing Continental culture; the slightly older Florio fascinating the playwright with tales of his travels, and of the latest developments in art and literature in Italy.

But there is evidence to suggest that, on the contrary, Shakespeare found Florio a garrulous bore. In his play *Love's Labours Lost*, the author seems to have intended the pedantic schoolmaster Holofernes as a portrait of Florio. Certainly the character quotes some lines of Italian poetry from Florio's Italian language manual, *Second Fruits* (1591). The speech from IV, 2 where these lines appear gives a flavour of Holofernes' multi-lingual ramblings. The 'Mantuan' is the Roman poet Virgil:

Fauste, precor gelida quando pecus omne sub umbra Ruminat,—and so forth. Ah, good old Mantuan! I may speak of thee as the traveller doth of Venice;

Venetia, Venetia,
Chi non ti vede non ti pretia.

Old Mantuan, old Mantuan! who understandeth thee not, loves thee not. Ut, re, sol, la, mi, fa. Under pardon, sir, what are the contents? or rather, as Horace says in his—What, my soul, verses?

Montaigne wrote an essay on cannibals, which of course appeared in Florio's translation of his *Essays*, not just because he had some ideas about cannibals and other natives of 'newly-discovered' lands, but also because he had acquired detailed information about a particular tribe which lived in the area of what is now Rio de Janeiro in Brazil.

The essayist, a wealthy nobleman, seems to have chosen some of his servants for rather whimsical reasons, and had a habit of talking to them at length, and finding them interesting. He describes one of these as (in Florio's translation) 'a simple and rough-hewn fellow: a condition fit to yield a true testimony'. What this man could testify about was the short-lived French colony of Antarctic France, in what is now Brazil, 'in that other world, which in our age was lately discovered . . . so infinite and vast a country' where he had lived 'for the space of ten or twelve years'. As well as just telling his master about the natives there, this man 'hath many times shown me diverse mariners, and merchants, whom he had known in that voyage'. Montaigne himself had had an opportunity to converse with some of these natives (through a frustratingly bad interpreter) in the French city of Rouen, 'in the time of our late King Charles the ninth'. The philosopher also had some tribal artefacts, and translations of songs sung by these natives.

The cannibals Montaigne wrote about in his essay would have been from one of the various Tupí tribes that then lived along the coast of what we now call Brazil. Although he seems to have taken a great interest in these people, and provides some detail about them in his essay, the conclusions he reaches about them and their way of life have more to do with his own philosophy than about how they actually lived. He sees them as youthful, happy children of nature, noble though savage, living in a world not unlike the ideal Golden Age of classical mythology. Even their enthusiastic consumption of their dead enemies he prefers to the torture of living enemies carried out by supposedly civilised European nations. He cites an example of cannibalism as practised among his own people, the French, in ancient times; and quotes the Roman poet Propertius on the virtues of natural things versus anything artificial:

Ivies spring better of their own accord,
Unhaunted plots much fairer trees afford.
Birds by no art much sweeter notes record.

One would think that Montaigne's ideas about the Tupí would have been applied by Shakespeare to his own cannibal, the 'savage and deformed' Caliban; but the playwright puts his own thinly-disguised version of Montaigne's sentiments into the mouth of Gonzalo, described as 'an honest old counsellor' in the play's *dramatis personae*. And Gonzalo isn't even describing the lives of the natives of Prospero's island, or anywhere else: he is describing how he would govern such an island if he were 'the king on't'. In fact his government would amount to deliberate anarchy, an attempt to restore his subjects to the 'natural' state lauded by Montaigne.

Gonzalo is one of a small group of learned but rather foolish and garrulous old men in Shakespeare's plays. Polonius in *Hamlet* is another example, and depending on how old he is supposed to be, Holofernes in *Love's Labours Lost* is another (and certainly the young page, Moth, calls Holofernes an old man). If Holofernes has something of John Florio in him, then it is likely that Gonzalo has as well. The fact that he practically quotes from Florio's Montaigne may be a pointer to a living, breathing source for this character.

As well as his celebrated translation of Montaigne's *Essays*, John Florio also published a translation of the voyages of the French explorer Jacques Cartier (1491-1557), called *A Short and Brief Narration of the Two Navigations and Discoveries to the Northwest Parts Called New France* (1580). Cartier had claimed what is now Canada for France, and some of his adventures resemble incidents in *The Tempest*. Some of the Native Americans he met mistook him for some sort of divine being, and in *The Tempest* Caliban temporarily thinks that the drunken butler Stephano is a god. The natives Cartier encountered tended to be good to him and his men at first, bringing them presents of food, but later they became a threat. This is just like Caliban, who initially loves Prospero, but later becomes his enemy and his slave.

The *Short and Brief Narration* and *The Tempest* are also similar in that both mention a variety of contrasting landscapes. Like Prospero's island, the east coast of North America as explored by Cartier has 'barren place and fertile' (Act I, scene 2).

Another narrative about the Americas that has long been regarded as a source for *The Tempest* is William Strachey's *True reportory of the wreck and redemption of Sir Thomas Gates Knight upon and from the islands of the Bermudas: his coming to Virginia, and the estate of that Colonie then, and after, under the government of the Lord La Warre*. As is often the case with such works, the full title, which doubles as what we would now call a blurb, tells the whole story.

One of Strachey's revelations is that the Bermudas, long thought to have been islands of deadly storms and demons, proved to be a place where, with a little ingenuity, shipwrecked European travellers could live pretty well. The 'still vex'd Bermoothes' are mentioned in I, 2 of *The Tempest*, but the only convincing link between Strachey's work and the play is Strachey's account of St Elmo's fire, which Shakespeare may have used, also in I, 2.

Commedia dell'arte, Virgil's *Aeneid,* Ovid's *Metamorphoses* and the Masque

The Commedia, mentioned briefly in the introduction to this book, was a popular type of theatrical comedy, originating in Italy. It thrived for some two hundred years, from about the middle of the sixteenth century. Commedia troops were small, and used minimal sets, and as such it was fairly easy for them to tour throughout Europe, and even to England.

Shakespeare seems to have known a lot about this particular type of performance, but if he ever saw Commedia actors performing, he may not have been able to follow their rapid, semi-improvised dialogue in Italian. To gain a real insight into what was being said, he would probably have needed an Italian speaker at his elbow, whispering the sense of the words to him in English. As a man fluent in both Italian and English, and with a knowledge of words from several Italian dialects, John Florio would have been the ideal interpreter, whether or not Shakespeare generally found him to be a tedious fellow.

Commedia performers used costumes, and sometimes masks, to help them represent one of a number of stock characters; including Pantalone, a comical old man, Zanni, a long-suffering servant, and Harlequin, a fore-runner of the modern circus clown. Other characters were not 'stock', and might be unique to the performance in hand.

Although the actors had a clear idea of the story they would be telling via their performance, their lines were not memorised from a written script, but rather semi-improvised. Performances would also include songs, dances and much physical 'business', some of it quite athletic.

Because there were no detailed scripts to write or print, we can't know exactly what Commedia actors said during their performances. The closest things to scripts or play-books that have been preserved are descriptions of performances, and 'scenarios': rough plots written down to remind the actors what they were supposed to do. Luckily, around a thousand of these scenarios have been preserved. One very practical aspect of them is the catalogue of stage properties needed to enact the story, which often comes straight after the *dramatis personae*.

Among the extant Commedia scenarios, there is one in particular that Kenneth Muir, in his book on Shakespeare's sources, picks out as a possible source for the plot of *The Tempest*. This is *Li Tre Satiri* or *The Three Satyrs*.

In *The Three Satyrs* the action is dominated by an unnamed magician who lives in a grotto, is angry at people who fail to show him respect, and who boasts of his magical powers, just like Prospero. Like Prospero, the magician's powers are bound up in a book – in *The Tempest*, Caliban attributes Prospero's power to *books*, plural:

> for without them
> He's but a sot, as I am, nor hath not
> One spirit to command: they all do hate him
> As rootedly as I. Burn but his books.

(III, 2)

Phillis, the nearest equivalent to Miranda in the *Three Satyrs* scenario, is turned into a tree as a punishment for her disobedience: in *The Tempest*, we learn that 'the foul witch Sycorax' who once dominated the island, used magic to trap Ariel inside a tree, as Prospero reminds that airy spirit in I, 2:

> she did confine thee,
> By help of her more potent ministers
> And in her most unmitigable rage,
> Into a cloven pine; within which rift
> Imprison'd thou didst painfully remain
> A dozen years

If Shakespeare ever saw *The Three Satyrs,* he might have got the impression that Phillis was supposed to be *trapped inside* the tree, not *turned into* a tree. Phillis also falls asleep by the power of magic, just like Miranda. Another character in *The Three Satyrs* is also trapped inside a rock, and a further character emerges from the mouth of a whale.

The equivalents to Caliban in *The Three Satyrs* are the eponymous satyrs themselves, 'wild men' who are not quite human and not quite animal, and can only be controlled by the magician's powerful book. Dancers disguised as satyrs appear in Shakespeare's

The Winter's Tale (IV, 4) which belongs to the same epoch of Shakespeare's output as *The Tempest*.

The shipwrecked characters in *The Three Satyrs* include Pantalone, the stock character of the comical old man, who is similar in some ways to Gonzalo, whose ramblings can sound a little ridiculous. Some of the survivors of the shipwreck dress up in stolen clothes, just like Stephano and Trinculo, and are mistaken for gods, as Caliban mistakes Stephano for a god, and as the Native Americans mistook Cartier for a deity.

Despite all these similarities, *The Three Satyrs* is not *The Tempest*. To begin with, the Commedia scenario doesn't take us to an unnamed island, but to Arcadia. The character of Phillis is not the magician's daughter, and, unlike Miranda, has no interest in men until her mind is changed by magic: she is a devotee of the goddess Diana, the chaste huntress.

Because *The Three Satyrs* happens in Arcadia, the land of pastoral mythology, there are shepherds living there, whereas Prospero's island has no human natives. The scenario also features a pagan temple, which has no equivalent in *The Tempest*.

When some characters in *The Three Satyrs* gain possession of the magician's book, they use it to summon up food for themselves, but are driven away when the book itself bursts into flames. In *The Tempest*, a rich banquet is presented to some of Prospero's enemies, then swept away before they can eat any of it. In this scene, Ariel appears dressed as a harpy, hinting at Shakespeare's knowledge of Book III of Virgil's *Aeneid*, where harpies snatch away food prepared for Aeneas and his companions. The *Aeneid* is also more directly referenced in II, 1 of *The Tempest*, where the shipwrecked courtiers discuss 'Widow Dido', Aeneas' royal African lover, who kills herself when Aeneas abandons her and leaves Carthage. Carthage, as Gonzalo explains, is now known as Tunis.

Ferdinand's first encounter with Miranda recalls some details of a meeting of the Trojan hero Aeneas and his mother in Book I of Virgil's *Aeneid*. Like Ferdinand, the shipwrecked son of the king of Naples in Shakespeare's *Tempest*, Aeneas has just arrived in a new land of which he knows little. He encounters what appears to be a beautiful maiden huntress, but as the son of a goddess he is able to detect something divine in this apparition. By contrast, Ferdinand thinks Miranda is a goddess. The unmarried, virginal, maiden state of the female in question is important in both passages. The disguised Venus also denies that she is a goddess, and Miranda denies that she is a 'wonder'. It is possible that the young actor playing Miranda was costumed as some kind of Amazonian huntress in the earliest performances of *The Tempest*.

Although Shakespeare may have been directly influenced by Virgil when he was writing this scene, he may have had a play by his contemporary, the playwright Christopher Marlowe, in mind. Marlowe's *Dido Queen of Carthage* is a short play, written by Marlowe for a company of child-actors, around the year 1593. Virgil's scene where Aeneas meets the disguised Venus is faithfully reproduced in Marlowe's Act I scene 1. Marlowe's Dido play may also have influenced Shakespeare's *Antony and Cleopatra*.

The Latin poet Ovid, who was a younger contemporary of Virgil, was much admired in ancient times, in the Middle Ages and in the time of Shakespeare; and his literary stock continues to be high today. His

Metamorphoses is a long series of verse-tales re-told from ancient mythology: as the title suggests, the connecting theme for the collection is metamorphosis – change and transformation, particularly of the magical variety. Ovid's treatment of the story of Medea in the *Metamorphoses* is not his only attempt to deal with the fascinating figure of Medea: she also featured in his *Heroides,* and in a play that is now lost.

The hero Jason comes away from the kingdom of Colchis on the Black Sea with the princess Medea as his new wife. Like Sycorax and Prospero in Shakespeare's play, she has command of powerful magic, which can seem scary even when it is being used for good.

Like Prospero and Sycorax, Medea finds herself in unfamiliar surroundings, but still able to use her powers. Sycorax was banished, Prospero was left for dead after his brother stole his dukedom, and Medea elopes with Jason.

Like Sycorax, Caliban and Ariel, Medea is a wild creature who seems to come from an age before civilisation. Like Prospero, and Oberon in Shakespeare's *A Midsummer Night's Dream*, Medea requires ingredients for her magical potions fetched from far-flung places. Whereas Ariel and Puck can fly of themselves to get these for their respective masters, Medea rides on a chariot pulled through the air by dragons.

In a passage from Arthur Golding's 1565 translation of the *Metamorphoses* that Shakespeare adapted for his own purposes, Medea invokes magical powers prior to working a terrifying spell on Jason's old father Aeson. Later, the spell actually works, and Aeson is transformed from an ailing old man to a man of about forty. Shakespeare mentions this spell in his *Merchant of Venice* (V, 1) where Jessica tells us that

> In such a night
> Medea gather'd the enchanted herbs
> That did renew old Aeson.

Like Medea, Jessica in *The Merchant* has turned her back on her own people to elope with a stranger: like Medea's Jason, Lorenzo's Jessica has brought him more treasure than just herself: Jason leaves Colchis with the golden fleece; and Jessica steals money and goods from her father Shylock's house.

As well as the Commedia, *The Tempest* owes something to another theatrical form of Shakespeare's time, the masque. In the English context, masques were extravagant productions staged at the royal court and at the homes of some lesser aristocrats. They combined music, dancing, poetry, drama and spectacular visual effects, and there was often an element of audience participation: the line between performers and audience was blurred, and aristocratic spectators would participate in dances, and even be given lines to speak.

The masques at the court of King James I could last over three hours, but they would only be performed once or twice, and were eye-wateringly expensive to put on. King James might pay as much as three thousand pounds for the staging of a masque; nearly three hundred thousand pounds today, or four hundred and fifty thousand U.S. dollars.

The best-known English masques of the seventeenth century were devised by the playwright and poet Ben Jonson together with the architect and designer Inigo Jones. Jonson's first masque was put on in 1603, and he continued to provide scripts for masques until long after Shakespeare's death in 1616; so it is likely that Shakespeare saw, or had read and/or heard of a number of these productions.

The Tempest features a short masque near the start of Act IV, where Prospero orders Ariel to call up spirits to provide the entertainment. This features the goddesses Ceres, Juno and Iris, and dancing nymphs and reapers, the latter in 'rye-straw hats'. All this is typical of the masques Jonson helped to devise, which often included mythological figures, and allegorical personages such as 'Truth', 'Opinion' and 'Love'.

As well as the short but elaborate masque in Act IV, the whole structure of *The Tempest* resembles that of a masque, in that the actions of Caliban, Stephano and Trinculo serve as the 'anti-masque', the comical mirror-image of the more formal part of a masque – a device which Jonson often deployed. The use of magic in *The Tempest*, and stage-effects such as Ariel appearing as a harpy, are consistent with the fantastical atmosphere of the typical masque.

In *Henry VIII*, a play Shakespeare wrote in collaboration with John Fletcher close to the time he wrote *The Tempest*, the eponymous king appears as a masquer with others 'habited like shepherds' (I, 4).

William Thomas: *History of Italy*

The Tempest may have been Shakespeare's last play, and anyone coming to it having first read all the other plays in the order in which they are thought to have been written will not be surprised that all the human characters are Italians.

Of the thirty-seven plays in the conventional Shakespearean canon, no less than thirteen are set wholly or partly in Italy: over thirty-five percent of the total. True, of these thirteen, five are set in, or have scenes in, ancient Rome, but Rome is of course an Italian city. A cursory reading of *Measure for Measure* might give the impression that it is the fourteenth play set in Italy, because so many of the characters have Italian names: Vincentio, Angelo, Claudio, even Shakespeare's 'other' Juliet; but in fact this play is set in Vienna.

It is clear that Shakespeare could have set some of his plays almost anywhere, but the fact is that the contemporary fascination with

Italy seems to have been such a 'draw' that the playwright was even tempted to sub-title *Othello* 'the moor of Venice'; though Othello himself isn't from Venice, and only one act of the play is set there. In Shakespeare's time both Italy and Italian were fashionable, which is one reason why John Florio was able to make a living from his knowledge of that language. Another man who wrote Italian language-books, though over twenty years earlier than Florio, was the Welshman William Thomas, who fled to Italy in 1545 as a fugitive from English justice.

Before he published his *Principle Rules of the Italian Grammar* in 1550, Thomas wrote the first English book about Italy: his *History of Italy*, which was published in 1549, and which was almost certainly known to Shakespeare. Despite the fact that the word 'history' appears in its title, Thomas's book has a lot to say about Italy, not as it was, but as he saw it when he lived there, from 1545 to 1548. Thomas was one of a long line of Brits who have been enchanted by Italy: its climate, its food, the architecture of its great cities and the elegance of its people.

The Italy of Thomas's time, and a long

time before and after, was the Italy of individual city-states, each of which had its own peculiar system of government. Thomas's sub-title to his book indicates its value as a description of a country which then acted as a kind of test-bed for different political systems: Thomas tells us that his book 'is exceeding profitable to be read because it entreateth of the state of many and divers commonwealths, how they have been and now be governed'.

In his description of the glories of Prospero's own city-state, Milan, Thomas hesitates to give the facts 'lest to him that never saw it I should seem overlarge in the due praising of it'; but he goes on to say that the city itself is 'honourable for the court, gallant for gentlemen, harbour for soldiers, delicate for dames, rich for merchants, and wealthy for artificers'.

Although there is much praise of many things Italian in his book, parts of his histories of the Italian city-states are sorry catalogues of regime-change by means of invasion, palace coups and 'popular uprisings' arranged by enemies of the current regime.

The name 'Prospero' appears in

Thomas's section on the fifteenth century history not of Milan, Prospero's city in *The Tempest*, but Genoa. A man called Prospero Adorno was declared duke of Genoa after a popular uprising, but was quickly expelled by the rival Fregoli family. He then returned, with military help from Milan, and became lieutenant for the Milanese in Genoa. After only a year, however, the Milanese suspected him of conspiring with Ferdinando, king of Naples, and, in Thomas's words, 'raised a new commotion of the people'. This 'commotion' failed to unseat Adorno: in fact it increased his power, and 'now he was made governor absolutely of the commonwealth'.

Various aspects of this story remind us of *The Tempest*: first, the name 'Prospero', and the name 'Ferdinando', which is just one letter longer than that of Ferdinand, Miranda's future husband in the play. Shakespeare's Ferdinand is the son of Alonso, the king of Naples, also a character in the play; and Thomas's phrase 'governor absolutely of the commonwealth' reminds us of Prospero's lines, referring to Antonio, his usurping brother: 'he needs will be | Absolute Milan'.

According to Prospero's account in the

play, the coup that unseated him took place at night, as he tells Miranda:

> Whereon,
> A treacherous army levied, one midnight
> Fated to th' purpose did Antonio open
> The gates of Milan, and, i' th' dead of darkness,
> The ministers for th' purpose hurried thence
> Me and thy crying self.

Shakespeare seems to have borrowed this night-time coup from an episode in Genoese history when an earlier Adorno, Barnabas, was deposed 'by force' by a usurper who 'entered by night into the city'.

Marlowe's *Doctor Faustus*

As we know, the English poet and playwright Christopher Marlowe was born in the same year as Shakespeare; but he died young from a wound sustained in a knife-fight in 1593, at the age of only twenty-nine. The fight is supposed to have followed an argument over 'the reckoning' (the check or bill) in a tavern, and it is meant to have prompted Shakespeare's reference to 'a great reckoning in a little room' in *As You Like It* (III, 3).

The Tragical History of the Life and Death of Doctor Faustus, which is thought to have been written in the 1590s, is perhaps Marlowe's most famous play. It tells the story of a German scholar, Faustus, who becomes fascinated by the 'metaphysics of magicians' and 'necromantic books' (I, 1). His studies enable Faustus to make a pact with the devil: he sells his soul in return for twenty-four years of unlimited power.

Although Faustus openly serves the devil, whereas Prospero tries to limit his magical activities to good causes, there are nevertheless many similarities between the two men. Both use books as sources of magical power and knowledge; and both neglect civic duties to spend more time on magic (Faustus was a famed physician and teacher in the German university town of Wittenberg, before he sold his soul). Prospero abandons his magic to return to his role as duke of Milan, and Faustus also takes a role in European politics, though he retains his magic powers.

Faustus is attended by good and bad angels, which could be seen as equivalents to

Ariel and Caliban, and he achieves much of his magic with the help of his attendant demon, Mephistopheles. Faustus has a strange affection for Mephistopheles, whose name is the last thing he cries out before he is dragged to hell at the end of the play. This may have suggested to Shakespeare the fatherly affection Prospero shows for Ariel. Like Ariel, Mephistopheles has a mischievous sense of humour, and can make himself invisible so as to play tricks on Faustus's victims. In one scene, magic is used to rob the pope of a rich banquet, a trick that is also played by Ariel on the shipwrecked courtiers in *The Tempest*.

In another of Faustus's stunts, he calls up 'a kennel of hounds' to attack a character called Benvolio, much as Prospero and Ariel deploy spirits disguised as dogs to frighten Stephano, Trinculo and Caliban (IV, 1). As with Prospero, one of the attractions of magic for Faustus is that he can use it to fetch rare items from all over the earth, including:

>   the treasure of all foreign wrecks,
> Yea, all the wealth that our forefathers hid
> Within the massy entrails of the earth.

(*Dr Faustus* I, 1)

Although rarities are fetched for him by Mephistopheles and other agents, Faustus is also able to travel through the air in a chariot drawn by dragons, like Ovid's Medea.

Like Prospero, Faustus uses his magical agents to summon spirits and make 'shows' to entertain or frighten his associates. Faustus presents us with Alexander the Great and his 'paramour' and, famously, with Helen of Troy (whom Faustus correctly calls 'Helen of Greece').

But Prospero is not Faustus, and Marlowe's play is not *The Tempest*. In Marlowe's play, Faustus uses his magical powers to increase his political influence and promote the cause of his native Germany (though initially he neglects his civic duties to spend more time with his magic books); whereas Prospero's immersion in magic causes him to lose his role as duke of Milan. Whereas Faustus is unable to abandon magic, burn his magic books and save his soul, Prospero does so, drowning his own books, and returning to Milan.

The two plays are also very different in structure, *Faustus* covering slightly more than the twenty-four years of Faustus's power, whereas the action of *The Tempest* is supposed to cover a mere three hours.

John Dee (1527-1608)

The appeal of plays like Marlowe's *Faustus* and Shakespeare's *Tempest* must have been enhanced for seventeenth century audiences by the fact that at that time many people still believed in what we would now class as magic. In those days, the dividing line between science and magic didn't really exist in the popular imagination.

On some days when Shakespeare's plays were being performed at Southwark, John Dee would have been in residence at his house at Mortlake, just over eleven miles to the west along the river Thames. Dee had a prodigious library at Mortlake, and was an accomplished mathematician and a renowned expert in the science of navigation; but his wide reading and his intellectual curiosity caused him to become 'rapt in secret studies' like Shakespeare's Prospero. Dee spent a lot of his time listening to the bizarre ramblings of his assistant Edward Kelley, who claimed to have contact with spirits, including one called Uriel, via a crystal ball or 'scrying glass' (Dee's 'glass' is now to be seen in the British Museum).

Among Dee's other investigations, he also looked into alchemy, and the promise of wealth and power that that subject held caused many important people, including the German emperor, the king of Poland, and Queen Elizabeth I, to take a serious interest in Dee's work.

Dee fell into disfavour during the reign of Elizabeth's successor, King James I. James was convinced that magic was real, and that adepts could indeed summon spirits; but he believed that such attempts were dangerous, and that all such spirits were demons. In his book *Daemonologie*, published in 1597, James warned that 'magicians' who used spirits and dabbled in magic were in fact consorting with Satan's agents:

. . . these forms, wherein Satan oblishes (binds) himself to the greatest of the magicians, are wonderful curious; so are the effects correspondent unto the same: for he will oblish himself to teach them arts and sciences, which he may easily do, being so learned a knave as he is:

to carry them news from any part of the world, which the agility of a spirit may easily perform . . .

In one passage, James addresses a specific delusion (as he sees it) of the magicians, who believe that certain types of spirits are harmless because (like Shakespeare's Ariel) they belong to fire and air, and have nothing of the baser elements about them (unlike Caliban, 'thou earth'):

. . . so they abuse the simplicity of these wretches, that becomes their scholars, that they make them believe, that at the fall of Lucifer, some spirits fell in the air, some in the fire, some in the water, some in the land: in which elements they still remain. Whereupon they build [argue], that such as fell in the fire, or in the air, are truer then they, who fell in the water or in the land . . .

In her books on Elizabethan occult philosophy, and on Shakespeare's last plays, Frances Yates argues that Shakespeare intended the character of Prospero as a kindly tribute to John Dee. Yates points out that the timing of this tribute was curious: by the time Shakespeare came to write this late play, Dee had probably already died, poverty-stricken and neglected, his posthumous reputation badly tarnished.

Prospero seems not to have any innate magical power, but is able to act magically through other beings and forces, deploying the power of his books: this is more or less how Dee must have regarded himself vis-a-vis magic, since he personally could not regularly see anything in his scrying glass, but relied on Kelley and other 'mediums'; much as Prospero relies on Ariel to do his bidding and to gather information.

Dee seems to have remained convinced that his studies had been lawful and that his spirits had not been demons; but at the end of *The Tempest* Prospero casts aside his 'rough magic'.

Kenneth Muir entertained the idea that Shakespeare may have known Dee personally, as a bibliophile and an antiquary, if not a wizard, but if he didn't, he would certainly have heard of him by reputation, and may have been familiar with some of his works. Dee's celebrated preface to Billingsley's 1570 English translation of Euclid's *Elements* is a re-statement of philosophical ideas that would have been familiar to Shakespeare from the general philosophical atmosphere of his time, which was pervaded by Neoplatonism, a philosophical school founded on the works of the Greek philosopher Plotinus (died 270 A.D.). One aspect of Neoplatonism was the belief that there was a mysterious level of reality that was only *reflected* by everyday reality, and that this mysterious domain could, under certain circumstances, be encountered, for instance through communication with spirits. In his preface to Euclid, Dee asserts that mathematics could serve as a link between these discrete realities:

[Mathematics] being (in a manner) middle, between things supernatural and natural, are not so absolute and excellent, as things supernatural: nor yet so base and gross, as things natural; but are things immaterial: and nevertheless, by material things able somewhat to be signified.

Yates asserts that, whereas Prospero represents an affectionate portrait of Dee, Marlowe's Faustus is quite the opposite. There is also a warning about the dangerous temptations of magic, particularly magical prophesy, in Shakespeare's *Macbeth*, a play that includes a character called Banquo, supposed to have been an ancestor of James I. A third way of depicting magic is to be found in Ben Jonson's comic play *The*

Alchemist, written at around the same time as *The Tempest*, in which Subtle, the equivalent of Dee, Prospero and Faustus, is a con-artist, using his supposed access to magical powers to deceive the innocent.

IV. Antony and Cleopatra

A knowledge of Virgil's *Aeneid* certainly informs the reader's understanding of Shakespeare's *Tempest*: it is also very relevant to a full appreciation of his *Antony and Cleopatra*.

With Troilus and Cressida and Romeo and Juliet, and the Venus and Adonis of Shakespeare's narrative poem, Antony and Cleopatra make up the fourth pair of famous star-crossed lovers about whom Shakespeare wrote.

As *Antony and Cleopatra* opens, the fledgling Roman empire is ruled by the three men of the so-called triumvirate – the young Octavius Caesar, Mark Antony himself, and Lepidus, a former ally of Julius Caesar. The play tells the story of how Antony's alliance with the Egyptian queen, Cleopatra, upsets the balance of power and leads to his military defeat and death. Shakespeare uses the fact that Antony and Cleopatra are lovers to raise issues about the pitfalls of love.

The story of Antony and Cleopatra, which, in Shakespeare's hands, grows from history into legend, is nevertheless historical, unlike the very similar story of Dido and Aeneas in Virgil's *Aeneid*, which Virgil attempts to turn from a remote legend into part of the history of the founding of Rome.

Like Cleopatra, Dido is a queen in Africa who is not, however, ethnically African. Dido was forced to flee her home city of Tyre (now Sur in modern Lebanon) and bought land in North Africa on which she founded the city of Carthage. Although Cleopatra was almost certainly born in Egypt, she was of the dynasty of the Ptolemies, Macedonian Greeks who ruled Egypt for nearly three hundred years. Shakespeare insists that Cleopatra is 'black' or 'tawny' like a 'gypsy'; but although she may have had some Egyptian blood, the portrait bust thought to be of her as a young woman (which is now at the Altes Museum in Berlin) looks extremely European.

Like Dido, Cleopatra falls for a hero who is likely to ruin his own destiny if he stays with her. Aeneas casts off Dido, who then kills herself; but Antony remains with

Cleopatra, a decision which brings him political and military disaster: eventually both of them commit suicide.

Antony, and of course Shakespeare himself, are both aware of the similarities between the two stories, and in Act IV scene 14 Antony imagines how he and Cleopatra will rival Dido and Aeneas in the afterlife:

Where souls do couch on flowers, we'll hand in hand,
And with our sprightly port make the ghosts gaze:
Dido and her Aeneas shall want troops,
And all the haunt be ours.

Although Dido is mentioned by name in no less than seven of Shakespeare's plays, he never wrote a play of his own about the tragic African queen. As we have seen in connection with *The Tempest*, the rival playwright Christopher Marlowe wrote *Dido, Queen of Carthage* at some time in the early 1590s, and some passages from this short play have echoes in *Antony and Cleopatra*.

When she is pleading with him to stay in Carthage with her, Marlowe's Dido tells the hero to 'speak like my Aeneas, like my love'. This is echoed in several passages in *Antony and Cleopatra*, particularly those where Antony appears not to be living up to his famous name. In III, 13, Cleopatra responds to Antony's rapid renewal of spirit with the words 'since my lord is Antony again | I will be Cleopatra.'

In IV, 4 of Marlowe's play, Dido shows some of the cruelty Cleopatra also displays:

Those that dislike what Dido gives in charge,
Command my guard to slay for their offence.
Shall vulgar peasants storm at what I do?

This recalls Cleopatra's treatment of the unfortunate messenger in III, 5:

What say you? Hence,
Horrible villain! or I'll spurn thine eyes
Like balls before me; I'll unhair thy head:
Thou shalt be whipp'd with wire, and stew'd in brine,
Smarting in lingering pickle.

In IV, 4 of *Dido, Queen of Carthage*, Dido is in a more tender mood:

It is Aeneas' frown that ends my days:
If he forsake me not, I never die ;

For in his looks I see eternity,
And he'll make me immortal with a kiss.

Readers familiar with Marlowe's *Doctor Faustus* will recognise 'make me immortal with a kiss', a phrase the playwright re-uses in Faustus's line 'Sweet Helen, make me immortal with a kiss', addressed to Helen of Troy; but the phrase 'in his looks I see eternity' is echoed in Cleopatra's reminiscence of the early days of her affair with Antony, in I, 3: 'Eternity was in our lips and eyes'.

As well as the similarities between the story of Dido and Aeneas and that of Antony and Cleopatra, the *Aeneid* is directly relevant to Shakespeare's play because a key episode in the lovers' story is related in Book VIII of Virgil's poem. Here Aeneas is given a shield by his mother, the goddess Venus, which has been forged by Vulcan, the blacksmith-god himself. The shield is decorated with scenes of the future glory of Rome, the city Aeneas is supposed to have founded. One of these scenes shows the turning-point of the battle of Actium, where Octavius, the future emperor Augustus, defeated Antony.

There is an unfortunate note of racism in Virgil's account of the battle. It is implied that the European victors are inherently superior to the eastern races who make up some of Antony's forces:

Rang'd on the line oppos'd, Antonius brings
Barbarian aids, and troops of Eastern kings;
Th' Arabians near, and Bactrians from afar,
Of tongues discordant, and a mingled war

(from John Dryden's translation, 1697)

A similar note is to be found in book ten of *The Civil War* (also known as the *Pharsalia*) by the later Roman poet Lucan. Here the poet describes how Julius Caesar fell for Cleopatra years before Mark Antony followed suit, blaming Julius's lapse on the fabled luxury and sensuality of the Egyptians, which is also a theme in Shakespeare's play:

His stubborn heart dissolves in loose delight,
And grants her suit for one lascivious night.
Egypt and Caesar now in peace agreed,
Riot and feasting to the war succeed;
The wanton queen displays her wealthy store,
Excess unknown to frugal Rome before.

(from Nicholas Rowe's translation, 1719)

Although many in Shakespeare's audience would have spotted, or had prior knowledge of, the similarities between the stories of Antony and Cleopatra, and Dido and Aeneas in Virgil, the main source of Shakespeare's play is not to be found in the works of the Roman poet, but in a book by the later Greek historian, Plutarch, who died around 120 A.D.

Plutarch's biography of Mark Antony is the longest of his *Parallel Lives*, a series of biographies, many of which he arranged in pairs of one Roman and one Greek subject, to allow him to make comparisons. Although the term 'Greek historian' may make him sound a little forbidding, Plutarch is a very readable and informal author. He mixes opinion, speculation and gossip with hard facts, humanising the subjects of his biographies by pointing up foibles and eccentricities, and not neglecting details such as their physical appearance and modes of dress and speech.

As a Greek (though also a Roman citizen) Plutarch could take a slightly disinterested view of characters like Mark Antony, Julius Caesar and Coriolanus, all of whom feature in his work and in plays by

Shakespeare.

Plutarch was born less than twenty years after the death of Mark Antony, and he tells us that his grandfather Lamprias had heard a tale about the goings-on in Antony's kitchens in Alexandria. It seems that one Philotas, a medical student and friend of Lamprias, visited these kitchens and saw vast quantities of food being prepared, including eight wild boars, although there were only twelve guests for supper. In Shakespeare's play (II, 2) these boars are mentioned in such a way that we assume that the twelve dinner guests went on to eat the whole lot:

MAECENAS
Eight wild-boars roasted whole at a breakfast, and but twelve persons there; is this true?

ENOBARBUS
This was but as a fly by an eagle: we had much more monstrous matter of feast, which worthily deserved noting.

but according to Plutarch, Antony's chefs cooked on an epic scale round the clock because they never knew when their master would want to eat.

Shakespeare used Plutarch as a source for *Julius Caesar*, *Coriolanus* and *Antony and Cleopatra*: his other Roman play, the seldom-performed *Titus Andronicus*, owes more to the Roman playwright and philosopher Seneca. Although it is one of Shakespeare's four Roman plays, *Antony and Cleopatra* is the only play that uses Egypt for a setting, something that has sometimes tempted theatre directors to costume Cleopatra as if she were, for example, Nefertiti, the famously beautiful wife of the eighteenth-dynasty pharaoh, Akhenaten.

But, as we have seen, Cleopatra ruled long after native Egyptians had ceased to govern their own country, and Shakespeare's Egypt has little to do with Akhenaten, Tutankhamen or the other native pharaohs whose lives have become known to us through modern archaeology and the decipherment of Egyptian hieroglyphs.

Shakespeare's Egypt is for the most part derived from Plutarch, and perhaps from the earlier Greek writer Herodotus, who visited Egypt in the fifth century before Christ. Herodotus's *Histories* would have been available to the playwright in an English translation published in 1584.

From Herodotus, Shakespeare might have learned many things that informed his understanding of ancient Egypt, including the idea that it was a country the history of which featured some powerful women, and where women played roles usually occupied by men, at least in Greek society. The perceived unnaturalness (particularly from the Roman and Greek point of view) of Antony's being ruled by a woman is another important theme in Shakespeare's play.

Herodotus, like Plutarch, had an eye for a good story, and many of his Egyptian tales are erotic in character. Of the pharaohs he mentions, Amasis and Mykerinos (the latter known as Menkaure to modern Egyptologists) share some characteristics with Shakespeare's Antony. Both were serious drinkers and revellers, and both thought it was perfectly reasonable for a ruler to behave in this way.

As well as Herodotus's account of Egypt, and Plutarch's *Lives*, Shakespeare may have known the latter author's short work *Concerning Isis and Osiris*. This may have been important for *Antony and Cleopatra*, as Cleopatra herself was known to dress up as Isis and to model herself on that goddess.

Plutarch's *Lives* was known to Shakespeare through the English translation by Thomas North (1579), a version that is still engaging and readable today.

A careful reading of North's account of Plutarch's Life of Antony not only reveals how much Shakespeare owed to this Elizabethan book: it also gives an insight into what Shakespeare had to do to turn North's prose narrative into a verse drama.

Even those parts of Plutarch's *Life of Antonius* that are relevant to the action of *Antony and Cleopatra* are much longer than a play can be; even one like *Antony and Cleopatra*, that can take over three hours to perform uncut.

A large stretch of Plutarch's Life deals with Antony's disastrous campaign against the Parthians, the people of an ancient kingdom in what is now Iran. This is relevant to his relationship with Cleopatra, because timing was all-important in ancient warfare, and Antony's preoccupation with the Egyptian queen caused him to rush the start of the campaign, and risk the total annihilation of his army. As North's Plutarch tells us:

For the earnest great desire he had to lie all winter with her made him begin his war out of due time, and for haste to put all in hazard, being so ravished and enchanted with the sweet poison of her love, that he had no other thought but of her, and how he might quickly return again, more than how he might overcome his enemies.

The resulting campaign involved movements of thousands of men who found themselves in a desperate state, in hostile environments, for long periods. As such the campaign would be difficult to dramatise even in the form of a Hollywood epic with a cast of thousands and a budget of tens of millions of dollars. For Shakespeare, with a cast of around twenty and a wooden 'cockpit' of a theatre at his disposal, it must have seemed wiser to do what he did – to limit the Parthian war to just a few mentions in the play. The one scene (III, 1) where Parthia is foregrounded has to do with the campaign not of Antony, but of Antony's deputy Ventidius against the Parthians, a campaign which preceded Antony's own. This scene is, however, nearly always cut from theatrical productions of the play.

Parthia is kept in the background of

Antony and Cleopatra partly for practical reasons, but this also helps to concentrate the play on the central drama of Antony's relationship with the Egyptian queen, who did not accompany him on his Parthian adventure. Another important piece of camouflage is Shakespeare's reduction of the importance of Octavia in the story. In Plutarch, Octavius's sister not only marries Mark Antony and bears him children – she also looks after his children by other women, takes care of his interests in Italy, and actively promotes peace and concord between her brother and her husband. After the death of Antony, she has an important role in looking after his surviving offspring. Partly because there is a limit to how long a play intended for performance in the Jacobean theatre could be, and partly, again, to sharpen his focus on the central lovers, Shakespeare only allows Octavia thirteen speeches (in contrast to over two hundred from Cleopatra); and she only appears in four of the play's forty-two scenes.

Cleopatra herself is also somewhat cut down in Shakespeare's play. She only appears in sixteen of the play's scenes, far less than Antony, who appears in twenty-two. Although she has slightly more speeches than Antony, she has far fewer words to say within those speeches. But she manages to dominate the play, 'punching above her weight', as it were, because other characters talk about her in scenes when she isn't onstage: the prime example of this is Enobarbus's famous description of her first meeting with Antony in Act II scene 2.

One reason why Shakespeare had to compress Cleopatra's part is of course that he had no female actors at his disposal, and had to rely on men and boys to play his women. In the case of Cleopatra, the playwright turns this preposterous limitation in theatrical logistics to his advantage, because her frequent absences from the stage, and the way we hear of her through the speeches of other characters, give Shakespeare's Egyptian queen an extra level of resonance and mystique.

Both Antony and Cleopatra have to be off-stage a lot during their own play because Shakespeare has inherited a complex story from Plutarch, which the playwright re-tells in an amazing cascade of forty-two scenes, some of which are very short. In this respect, *Antony and Cleopatra* contrasts with *Richard III*, which has twenty-five scenes, and *The Tempest*, which has only nine. The scenes in *Antony and Cleopatra* are also set in a bewildering number of locations, including not just several places in Rome, and Alexandria in Egypt, but also Misenum (now Miseno in Italy), Syria, Athens, and Actium (in Greece).

The complexity of the story of the ill-fated lovers has tempted some playwrights to compress the action of their plays on Antony and Cleopatra to just a few hours. In plays by Mary Herbert, Samuel Daniel and John Dryden we see the characters at the end of their story, reflecting on what has gone before. This is like the approach of Greek and Roman tragedy, and also like *The Tempest*, where Prospero's early speeches summarise many years of action.

Despite the complex story he has to tackle, Shakespeare doesn't use a formal chorus or even a prologue in *Antony and Cleopatra*. Instead, the playwright gives us a character called Philo, who opens the play with fourteen lines about how Antony's obsession with Cleopatra has caused his decline. Apart from three lines near the end of this scene (I, 1) Philo never speaks again.

Much of the rest of the semi-detached commentary, description and explanation we need to help us through the play comes from the mouth of Enobarbus, who, like Plutarch himself, has mixed feelings about the play's hero. According to John Wilders in his introduction to the 1995 Arden edition of the play, part of the function of Enobarbus is to stand in for Plutarch as narrator.

As well as replacing the narrative voice of Plutarch, excluding much of Antony's Parthian campaign, stripping down Octavia, and making Cleopatra a manageable part for a young boy, Shakespeare excludes some of the nastier aspects of the characters of Antony and Cleopatra, as they are represented in Plutarch.

As a world leader, Antony had ample scope for nastiness on a grand scale. During his unfortunate campaign against the Parthians, Antony punished his own troops by decimating them: that is to say, he slaughtered one in ten of them, choosing the victims by a kind of ghastly lottery. Plutarch also tells us that Antony's expenditure in both war and peace was so great that he had to impose cruelly excessive taxes:

In the end he doubled the taxation, and imposed a second upon Asia. But then Hybreas the orator, sent from the estates of Asia to tell him the state of their country, boldly said unto him: 'If thou wilt have power to lay two tributes in one year upon us, thou shouldst also have power to give us two summers, two autumns, and two harvests.'

As for the Egyptian queen, whereas Shakespeare merely tells us that 'She hath pursued conclusions infinite | Of easy ways to die', Plutarch tells us exactly how she investigated suicide techniques:

Cleopatra in the meantime was very careful in gathering all sorts of poisons together to destroy men. Now, to make proof of those poisons which made men die with least pain, she tried it upon condemned men in prison. For, when she saw the poisons that were sudden and vehement, and brought speedy death with grievous torments, and, in contrary manner, that such as were more mild and gentle had not that quick speed and force to make one die suddenly: she afterwards went about to prove the stinging of snakes and adders, and made some to be applied unto men in her sight, some in one sort and some in another. So, when she had daily made divers and sundry proofs, she found none of all them she had proved so fit as the biting of an aspic [asp], the which only causeth a heaviness of the head, without swounding or complaining, and bringeth a great desire also to sleep, with a little sweat in the face, and so by little and little taketh away the senses and vital powers, no living creature perceiving that the patients feel any pain. For they are so sorry when anybody waketh them, and taketh them up, as those that being taken out of a sound sleep are very heavy and desirous to sleep.

We have seen how Cleopatra modelled herself on the Egyptian goddess Isis: Antony also had a god for a role-model, the god Hercules, from whom he believed he was descended – indeed his name, Antony, was supposed to have been derived from that of Anton, a son of Hercules. Hercules is mentioned four times in the play, once by the name 'Alcides' when, at IV, 12, Antony is reminding himself that he is a descendant of the god. At IV, 3 soldiers guarding Cleopatra's palace at Alexandria hear a strange sound which one of them takes to be 'the god Hercules, whom Antony loved' deserting him. In Plutarch's version of this strange event, there is a lot more detail about what is heard (Shakespeare merely gives us the sound of 'hautboys', or oboes, under the stage):

Furthermore, the self same night within little of

midnight, when all the city was quiet, full of fear and sorrow, thinking what would be the issue and end of this war: it is said that suddenly they heard a marvellous sweet harmony of sundry sorts of instruments of music, with the cry of a multitude of people, as they had been dancing, and had sung as they use in Bacchus' feasts, with movings and turnings after the manner of the satyrs: and it seemed that this dance went through the city unto the gate that opened to the enemies, and that all the troop that made this noise they heard went out of the city at that gate. Now, such as in reason sought the depth of the interpretation of this wonder, thought that it was the god unto whom Antonius bare singular devotion to counterfeit and resemble him, that did forsake them.

The fact that Shakespeare substitutes Hercules for Bacchus here may be another example of his simplifying the story: Plutarch tells us that Antony emulates both Bacchus and Hercules – Shakespeare tries to streamline this and avoid unnecessary ambiguity.

Wilders reminds us of an ancient story about Hercules, in which he is made effeminate by the love of Omphale and forced to wear women's clothes; and another where he has to make a choice between virtue and vice. In the latter story, re-told in the Greek writer Xenophon's *Memorabilia*, the female personification of Virtue addresses her counterpart, Vice, in terms that recall the luxurious life Antony has fallen into:

Thou, that mayest not even await the desire of pleasure, but, or ever that desire springs up, art already satiated; eating before thou hungerest, and drinking before thou thirsteth; who to eke out an appetite must invent an army of cooks and confectioners; and to whet thy thirst must lay down costliest wines, and run up and down in search of ice in summer-time; to help thy slumbers soft coverlets suffice not, but couches and feather-beds must be prepared thee and rockers to rock thee to rest; since desire for sleep in thy case springs not from toil but from vacuity and nothing in the world to do. Even the natural appetite of love thou forcest prematurely by every means thou mayest devise, confounding the sexes in thy service. Thus thou educatest thy friends: with insult in the night season and drowse of slumber during the precious hours of the day.

(trans. H.G. Dakyns, 1897)

Afterword: Sources for the Sources

Anyone writing an introduction to the sources of Shakespeare's plays owes a huge debt of gratitude to the researchers who have gone before, among whom the towering figures are Geoffrey Bullough and Kenneth Muir. Muir in his *Sources of Shakespeare's Plays* (1977) and Bullough in his eight-volume *Narrative and Dramatic Sources of Shakespeare* (the last volume of which was published in 1975) reviewed previous work in the field, made new discoveries and, in Bullough's case, printed lengthy extracts from the sources.

It must be remembered that Bullough, Muir and their predecessors were working without the benefit of digital technology, which now makes it possible, for instance, to search all of Shakespeare's works for his use of a particular word in seconds. Bullough and Muir were working from concordances and, no doubt, index cards and piles of physical books and scholarly journals: this makes their achievement even more remarkable.

As well as Muir and Bullough, generations of editors of the Arden editions of Shakespeare's works have also sifted through, and reproduced, a range of Shakespearean sources, as have the editors of the Norton critical editions, and the inexpensive Signet Classic Shakespeare, where the current author first encountered extracts from the sources.

Bibliography

For sixteenth and seventeenth century texts in the bibliography below, the name of the printer is sometimes placed where the publisher would normally appear, since the role of printer and publisher was often filled by the same person. Editions of Shakespeare's plays are only included where those plays are examined in detail: see also 'Shakespeare Plays Mentioned in the Text' below.

Books

Ackroyd, Peter: *Shakespeare: The Biography*, Random House, 2006

Akrigg, G.P.V.: *Shakespeare and the Earl of Southampton*,Hamish Hamilton, 1968

Aubrey, John: *Aubrey's Brief Lives: A*

Selection, Langley Press, 2014

Aubrey, John: *Aubrey's Brief Lives: The Elizabethans*, Langley Press, 2014

Baldwin, David: *Richard III*, Amberley, 2013

Bryson, Bill: *Shakespeare: The World as a Stage*, Harper, 2012

Bullough, Geoffrey: *Narrative and Dramatic Sources of Shakespeare*, Volume III, Routledge, 1960

Bullough, Geoffrey: *Narrative and Dramatic Sources of Shakespeare*, Volume V, Routledge, 1964

Bullett, Gerald (ed.): *Silver Poets of the Sixteenth Century*, Everyman, 1947

Burgess, Anthony: *Shakespeare*, Cape, 1970

Campbell, Lily B (ed.) *The Mirror for Magistrates*, Cambridge, 1938

Casaubon, Meric (ed.): *A true & faithful relation of what passed for many years*

between Dr John Dee and some spirits . . .
D. Maxwell, 1659

Dee, John: *The Diaries of John Dee*, Day, 1998

Dee, John: *Essential Readings*, Crucible, 1986

Dryden, John: *All For Love*, Nick Hern, 1998

Erickson, Carolly: *Brief Lives of the English Monarchs*, Constable, 2007

Euclid: *Elements* [translated by Henry Billingsley, with a preface by John Dee], John Daye, 1570

Frame, Donald M: *Montaigne: A Biography*, Hamish Hamilton, 1965

Grant, Raymond J.S.: *Laurence Nowell, William Lambarde, and the Laws of the Anglo-Saxons*, Rodopi, 1996

Greene, Robert: *Greene's Groats-worth of Wit, Bought with a Million of Repentance*, William Wright, 1592

Guy, John: *Thomas More*, Arnold, 2000

Hall, Edward: *Hall's Chronicle*, London, 1809

Halliday, F.E.: *A Shakespeare Companion: 1564-1964*, Penguin, 1964

Haslewood, Joseph (ed.) *Mirror for Magistrates*, London, 1815

Herodotus: *The History of Herodotus* translated by G.C. Macaulay, Macmillan, 1890

Hicks, Michael: *Edward IV*, Arnold, 2004

'James R' [King James I]: *Daemonologie*, Robert Waldegrave, 1597

Jonson, Ben: *The Complete Masques*, Yale, 1969

King Darius, Hugh Jackson, 1577

Logan, George M. (ed.): *The Cambridge Companion to Thomas More*, Cambridge, 2011

Lucan: *The Civil War*, Translated by
Nicholas Rowe, Everyman, 1998

Machiavelli, Niccolo: *The Prince*, Penguin,
2003

Mackay, Charles: *Extraordinary Popular
Delusions and the Madness of Crowds*,
Wordsworth, 1995

Marlowe, Christopher: *The Complete Plays*,
Penguin, 1969

Meres, Francis: *Palladis Tamia*, P. Short,
1598

Miola, Robert S.: *Shakespeare's Reading*,
Oxford, 2000

Montaigne, Michel de: *Essays*, Penguin,
1958

More, Thomas: *The History of King Richard
III*, Langley Press, 2015

Muir, Kenneth: *The Sources of
Shakespeare's Plays*, Methuen, 1977

Mukherji, Subha and Lyne, Raphael: *Early Modern Tragicomedy*, D.S. Brewer, 2007

Munro, Lucy: *Archaic Style in English Literature, 1590-1674*, Cambridge, 2013

Nice Wanton, John King, 1560

Noble, Richmond: *Shakespeare's Biblical Knowledge*, SPCK, 1935

Oreglia, Giacomo: *The Commedia dell'arte*, Methuen, 1968

Ovid: *Metamorphoses* translated by Arthur Golding, Penguin, 2002

Ovid: *Selected Works*, Everyman, 1939

Paterson, Don: *Reading Shakespeare's Sonnets: A New Commentary* Faber & Faber, 2012

Plutarch: *Shakespeare's Plutarch*, edited by T.J.B. Spencer, Penguin, 1964

Pope, Joseph: *Jacques Cartier, His Life and Voyages*, Ottawa, 1890

Pound, Ezra: *ABC of Reading*, Faber, 1951

Rowse, A.L.: *The England of Elizabeth*, Reprint Society, 1953

Shakespeare, William: *Antony and Cleopatra*, Routledge, 1995

Shakespeare, William: *Antony and Cleopatra*, Norton, 2011

Shakespeare, William: *Henry IV Part II*, Methuen, 1966

Shakespeare, William: *King Richard III*, Methuen, 1981

Shakespeare, William: *King Richard II*, Methuen, 1961

Shakespeare, William: *The Sonnets*, Everyman, 1993

Shakespeare, William: *The Tempest*, Arden, 1999

Shakespeare, William: *The Tempest*, Norton, 2004

Skidmore, Chris: *Bosworth: The Birth of the Tudors*, Phoenix, 2014

Staden, Hans: *Hans Staden's True History*, Duke University Press, 2008

Thomas, William: *The History of Italy*, Cornell, 1963

Virgil, *The Aeneids of Virgil Done Into English Verse,* by William Morris, Longmans, 1900

Xenophon: *The Works of Xenophon*, translated by H.G. Dakyns, Macmillan, 1897

Yates, Frances A.: *The Occult Philosophy of the Elizabethan Age*, Ark, 1983

Yates, Frances A.: *Shakespeare's Last Plays: A New Approach*, Routledge, 1975

Journal Articles

Dawson, Giles E.: *A Seventh Signature for Shakespeare,* Shakespeare Quarterly, Vol. 43, No. 1 (Spring, 1992), pp. 72-79

Ure, Peter: *Shakespeare's Play and the French Sources of Holinshed's and Stow's Account of Richard II*, Notes and Queries, October, 1953

Plays and Poems Written Wholly or Partly by William Shakespeare Mentioned in the Text

Antony and Cleopatra
As You Like It
Coriolanus
Cymbeline
Hamlet
Henry IV Parts I and II
Henry V
Henry VI parts I, II & III
Henry VIII
King John
Love's Labours Lost
Macbeth
The Merchant of Venice
Pericles
Richard II
Richard III
Romeo and Juliet
Sir Thomas More
The Tempest

Troilus and Cressida
The Winter's Tale

Poems

Sonnets
The Rape of Lucrece
Venus and Adonis

For free downloads and more from the
Langley Press, please visit our website at:
http://tinyurl.com/lpdirect